Before I Was Me

by

P.B. Castle

ISBN-13:   9798726124896

There IS hope!

Thanks to:

Dad for believing
Mom for forgiving
Husband for loving
Daughter for supporting
Myself for trusting

And because I am a survivor, to all the women who have lived, or died, or are still surviving with domestic violence, this story – my story – is dedicated to you because there is hope.

Chapter 1

Sitting down ...

I begin writing as though I am sitting across the table at a café with you, sharing my story. It's raw, it's real, and I tell things as I can best remember them. This account is not necessarily in any type of order, but I have tried to keep it as close as possible to the chronology of events as they happened.

I have wanted to write this story down for over twenty years but I have never really had the patience or the confidence to do so.

Then, one day, I felt that it was time.

I love to walk every day, and while I walk, I pray. It is my precious time to talk with my Father in Heaven, to honor Him, and to go to Him with my concerns, my needs and my gratitude.

He is the reason I was able to sit down and begin this journey when I did. As I walked, I asked Him for guidance, to open my mind to the things that needed to be shared in this story in order to help others, in order to help you. The reason for this book is not just to tell my story after all this time, but to serve a purpose, a much higher one, hopefully, that will touch your heart.

Whether you are a survivor yourself or are currently in an abusive relationship, we are all God's children and He loves each and every one of us and knows us intimately. He is the reason I can sit and write this down today. He is the reason I reached deep within me and drew from the strength I did not even know I had when things got really, really bad. He is the one who has gotten me through every trial, heartbreak and betrayal I have had to endure. He is also the one who has blessed me with everything I have ever needed, and continues to do so.

It is to Him that I dedicate this book. I hope you can draw strength, courage and hope from my story.

Thank you for getting this far.

Chapter 2

Beginnings

Hi, my name is P, and I am a domestic violence survivor.

Let me ask you a question:

Do you remember the very first time you got hit or slapped? Do you remember the first time you were verbally or emotionally abused? How about the first time he said he would *never* do it again?

I grew up in an affluent community in a good neighborhood where all of us went to the same K-12 school. Most of the families in my neighborhood knew each other. The men worked at the local copper mine, while moms were teachers, nurses or stay-at-home moms. My father was a mining director, and my mom had been a teacher and a substitute teacher at times, but I don't recall her teaching once I came along.

You see, it took my parents many years to have me. My mother wanted six kids, but she kept having miscarriages owing to a history of severe female reproductive issues and complications. So, after years of trying on their own, they began to consider adoption. Then, one day, my mom was pregnant, with me.

While I was born in the late 60s in Arizona, my parents had been living in Mexico, not too far past the Mexican border. Because travel between Mexico and the USA was quite different back then, my mom was able to give birth to me here in the USA. When she recovered enough to go home, we went back to Mexico. I was less than a week old.

I loved growing up in Mexico. I still, to this day, love the culture, the rich history, the people and their simple ways of living (and don't forget the food!).

Geographically, it's beautiful and diverse, and the people truly are hospitable, warm and loving. "Mi casa es su casa," as I'm sure you know, means "My house is your house," and we mean it. You will never feel like a stranger in a Mexican home, and I still embrace this philosophy in my own home to this day.

"Welcome! Mi casa es su casa!"

I mention some of these things to give you an idea of what influenced me as I was growing up, and the ideals, standards and expectations I was raised with. I want to give you an inside look at my life and how I became a victim and a survivor of domestic violence to show you that this plague does not discriminate, that it will see itself through to anyone regardless of race, color, creed, age, social upbringing, financial or religious status. It doesn't matter if you live in the USA, Mexico, or any other part of the world, or in a trailer, a boat, a truck or a mansion: someone will be affected by it. Whether it's you reading this book now, or someone you know, there is always somebody of whom we can unfortunately say, "Yes, I know, knew, or am that somebody," a victim of domestic violence.

I had many friends growing up and had a decent childhood. I went to a good school and wanted to be a lawyer. But when I was nine years old, we had to move down to Southern Mexico for my dad to take on a new job. It was difficult at first to leave all my friends behind and attend a new school, but in time, and with my mom's help, I made new friends. I kept in touch with several of my friends back home by the form of correspondence which is now so sweetly referred to as "snail mail."

One friend in particular was very dear to me. I would receive a letter from him every week and it was lovely. We are still friends to this day.

This went on for about three years, when my dad once again had to move for work. We moved back to Northern Mexico, this time several hours away from where I grew up, but it was still Mexico, and this time we were moving to the beach!

I was twelve.

Back in the late 1960s, my father had drawn up, designed and built a beautiful beach house for his parents. It was intended for all in the family to enjoy, but was primarily for my grandparents to get away in winter from Northern Arizona and warm up a bit.

Many memories and good times were shared by the family in this home, including my grandparents' fiftieth wedding anniversary. We have wonderful memories captured, frozen in time, by pictures taken of that day. I love to look at them because I see my grandparents surrounded by friends and family, and my parents so young and full of life, smiling and looking so happy.

(I don't know where I was at that time as I am not in any of those pictures.)

All in all, we had a normal, happy family and a seemingly a happy life.

In 1982, we moved to the beach house. It had been left to my father when my Grandpa passed away several years before. I am amazed at how God's timing always works in our lives, because this was the only home we had to go to when my dad changed jobs. In fact, I recall him having to drive about an hour to work each time he had to go.

The village we moved to was a small one. There were not many supplies or things to do. There was only one doctor in the village and one main street. But the people were welcoming, friendly, and genuine. Although we had visited this village numerous times while I was growing up, we now lived here. It was going to be great. We were living by the beach and I love the beach.

Let me tell you why I have such a passion for it. I picture the ocean and its great power as the very breath of God, inhaling and exhaling, His breath is captured in the waves of a stormy day or in its mirror finish on a quiet, calm and sunny morning, as if God is sitting back, relaxing and taking in His amazing creation.

To me, God has always been a huge part of my life, and I have always felt His presence by the ocean. I am also in awe of the glorious array of colors of those sunsets I could never get enough of. It was as if I could take in a deep breath and feel the warmth of the sun flow through my body as the sun set, soaking up an inner calm.

I recall sitting on our porch one morning, facing the beautiful blue, clear water, sipping on my morning brew, when a school of dolphins swam by. They headed east in the morning, as if they were keeping guard of our bay during the day, and then swam home to the west in the evening. I would imagine them heading home after a long day of pleasurable work, keeping the bay free of sharks and other sea critters that were afraid of dolphins. It makes me smile just remembering this as I write it down.

This scene happened many times over.

On one occasion, my dad came out with his binoculars. He was very particular about his binoculars. They had to be handled with much care and I had to put them right back into their case when I was done. I guess this was one way for him to instil responsibility in me. It later became standard to keep them close by to look out for the dolphins in the morning.

I asked to borrow them as I saw something dark way out in the water, but I wasn't sure if it was our dolphin friends or not. As I focused in on the image, I noticed that it was indeed the dolphins, but they looked a little different today.

As I continued to focus on that remarkable image, I found myself staring at an amazing sight. I saw the mom dolphins tossing their babies up in the air ever so gently, flipping them and teaching them how to continue on their own. Wow! It seemed as though they were flying three or four feet in the air, flipping and twirling like acrobats over the water, then splashing down, playing and smiling when they hit the clear blue water. What a great thing to experience. What a blessing to witness yet another precious creation of God and have that event permanently etched into my memory. I am so grateful.

I lived in this paradise of white sandy beaches, clear blue water, incredible sunsets, fresh salty air, crazy seagulls, and fishing boats against the horizon.

Then, one day, I met him.

Chapter 3

Him

I was almost fifteen years old and completely innocent. I had never even thought about having a boyfriend. All my 'boy' friends up until that point were either neighborhood friends or school mates. Feeling romantic about a boy was entirely new to me.

But this boy was so handsome and so cute. And he worked at the only local post office in our village, and he even held an official position there.

And he had a car and an apartment!

(And did I mention that he was cute, so cute, and that he smelled good and that he dressed well?)

He also seemed very smart and he had great hair. He had to be nice, he had to be smart, right? After all, he was so cute.

Occasionally, my dad had business to take care of in our village and I insisted that I go with him. I insisted that Dad take me with him just so I could see him, although I didn't tell him that.

I was just a teenager, and this guy was too, so what could ever come of it? I just wanted to see him. He looked so good.

So my dad would let me go with him, not even knowing why I wanted to go, and there I would sit next to the desk where my dad was doing his transactions and just watch this guy, then look away as soon as he moved so he wouldn't notice me staring at him.

What if I had been caught staring? I would have been mortified. Would he see through my sweet, naïve eyes the crazy crush I had developed for him, or would he see a lovesick, crazed little girl who should be home playing with her dolls instead?

Who cared, as long as I didn't get caught staring at him.

This went on for weeks.

During this same time, my best pen pal I spoke of earlier came to visit me for two weeks. We were like two peas in a pod and had such a good time together. We played on the beach, ran, swam, ate, and drove around the neighborhood. We made great childhood memories that I still treasure to this day. This friend calls me at Christmas and always on my birthday, and we'll reminisce on those memories, laughing and remembering what it was like to be free, to be a child with no worries, no responsibilities. Back when life was so simple. He is now a great doctor in Texas.

One day, my dad asked us to go into the village and take some papers in for him to where the guy worked. When you grow up in a small village, one of the perks is you get to drive at a younger age (fourteen in my case), so my friend and I drove everywhere. But on this day we had to go there, where he was – the guy, that oh-so-cute guy!

I had to get prepped to make sure I looked good and smelled good, to make sure I would catch his eye when I had to walk in and handle my father's business affairs.

So off we went …

I don't remember what happened after we walked in that day, mainly because it was so long ago, but I must have said something or acted in a way that made my friend upset at me, because all I can remember of that occasion is that, after we had finished our business there and were getting ready to walk out, my friend slapped me on the shoulder and called me a "coqueta," a flirt.

I can't recall much in the sense of day-to-day events during those two weeks, only that my friend and I enjoyed the last few remaining days together doing what we did best – getting into trouble (just a little) and making great memories.

One day we had this brilliant idea to hike up the tallest mountain in the village. It's actually a dead volcano that stands at the end of the road with the ocean on the other side.

What a sight it was once we reached the top. We were surrounded by the ocean everywhere, and from that height the water looked like a beautiful pool of teal and turquoise swirls. Amazing!

Now, the geography of this mountain is a little tricky as it is made up of mainly loose cinders and cactuses, and it towers about one hundred feet high. Going up was not a problem, but coming down was another story. I panicked. I was paralyzed. I could not move. And it was time to go back home.

My friend put his hands on my shoulders and shook me, not too hard but enough to get my attention. He told me we had to get down, that we had no other choice.

It was nearing noon and getting very hot and humid. He started down this loosely graveled slope, holding his hand out for me to follow. Next thing I knew, we were down. What an exhilarating, daring, and memorable experience.

Eventually the day arrived when my friend had to go home. We continued to write to each other and exchange an occasional phone call, but I would not see him again for almost twenty years.

The local school was just for local kids and was not an American school. In previous cities in which we had lived, I had attended the American schools which were provided primarily to American workers' families.

We tried to adapt to the Mexican school system when I entered the fifth grade, but the curriculum was so different from what I had experienced before that I simply couldn't manage it. I understood the language just fine, but I could not understand the subjects.

I was now in seventh grade and my mom taught me at home through a series of correspondence classes over the next three years.

My mom's previous teaching experience played a huge role in my life here. I don't believe in coincidences but in God's timing, again very important to me and in my life, as you will see later on.

One afternoon I was sitting on the top of our beautifully decorated masonry fence in our front yard, facing the desert across the street. I sat on that ledge many, many times over the summer. I liked to watch the cars go by and just enjoy the feel of the light breeze. Tall palm trees in our front yard shaded me from the hot sun, which was nice as temperatures could go past one hundred degrees, with high humidity, in the summer.

Birds were chirping and I could hear the ocean waves as they made it to shore in the background. My mom's lovely array of mixed and brightly colored tropical flowers was scattered throughout the yard, providing resting spots for butterflies and hummingbirds alike. What a peaceful setting to sit and enjoy nature.

All of a sudden I heard music, but couldn't make out the car from which it was coming until it got closer. Then I noticed it was him! You know, *him!*

I can still hear that 80s song loudly blaring out of his car as he drove by.

The car was unique in color. Because we were in a small village, not very many people had cars, so his was the only one of its kind. In a small village you quickly learn the different sounds of cars, trucks, and buses, and who drives them. In time I would eventually make out his sound and know he was driving home as he passed by on the main road in front of our home.

Sometimes I would hear him during the lunch hour or in the mornings on his way to work. Sometimes it was on a weekend, although that was rare as he frequently left town. Either way, I could be inside, and, if the windows were open, I could tell he was driving by.

I can only assume that, as many times as I sat on that fence and as many times as he drove by, he must have seen me too. On one occasion, he actually stopped and said, "Hi."

I don't remember anything after that. I assume I also said, "Hi," and we introduced ourselves to each other. I have chosen not to mention his name ever in these writings, but will simply refer to him as "X."

The very next thing I can recall is us seeing each other on a regular basis. Were we a couple? Were we really boyfriend and girlfriend, or was that just my perception?

X started calling on me, mainly in the early evenings. He mentioned that he was nineteen. Much later I found out that he was actually older, but by then it was too late.

The first time X came over and stayed a while, my mother was in the kitchen, which was directly in front of the living room. This is where we kept our AM/FM 8-track cassette record player my grandmother had given us for Christmas. There was no TV and, before this life-saving, glorious stereo came to be, we only had an ugly AM radio that I had learned to tune just slightly off broadcast to make it sound better. I would dance, listening to it daily with my mom, usually during the evenings while my dad was away at work, or in the middle of the day as mom prepared lunch.

In fact, it was while listening to this radio that I heard of 'The Sally Jesse Raphael Show' for the very first time and became hooked. I looked forward to her broadcast every morning after that. Years later I discovered she had a TV show and I would watch it every chance I got until she retired.

X brought with him a fancy new VHS video recorder and filmed a large portion of our first date, mainly to test the recorder out and to play with this new toy. My mom made a beeline back to the kitchen after a short cameo appearance she had not expected. That tape existed for many years to come, although now I have no idea where it is.

X and I were listening to his cassette tape of mixed 80s songs while talking. We even did a little dancing. I sat on one end of our 70s orange sectional and he sat on the other. I was wearing jeans and had borrowed my dad's very oversized, long-sleeve, rust-colored sweater with a wide black patent belt around my tiny waist. I wore boots over my jeans and had long, feathered sun-bleached hair. My skin was smooth and tan. I wore glasses and I had gotten braces just a few months before.

After a few hours, it got dark outside. My mom and I walked X to the door and bid him goodnight, and he left.

For many weeks thereafter, he stopped by in the mornings for a cup of coffee before going to work. Sometimes he came in for lunch as well.

Chapter 4

Innocence lost

The very first time I went out on a real date with X, we went with another couple from the village. They were friends with X and had a boat with water skis, and they invited us to join them on the other side of that tall mountain I mentioned earlier, the one I couldn't get down from right away.

On the other side of that mountain was a very private stretch of beach, narrow and covered with small mesquite bushes. The men set up the boat and skis while we women set up the towels and such on the beach beneath the bushes for shade.

We watched as they took turns in the water.

After a while, the other guy took his wife for a short boat ride around the bay, and X and I were left alone on the beach.

I remember feeling nervous, excited, and a little frightened as there was no one around and all I could hear was the faint sound of the boat's engine in the distance. Occasionally a seagull flew by, singing as they do in hope of finding a dead, washed-up fish on the beach, or to bully another bird's meal away from it. Seagulls are scavengers and lazy; if they don't have to hunt themselves for food, then they won't.

I never realized the irony of that scene until now, looking back on that day.

X had gotten up and waded into the ocean, which at this time in the morning was calm and reflective, like walking into a mirror.

He invited me in and I, hesitantly, knowing it would still be chilly, walked toward the shore. I sheepishly waded in until I was standing next to him, about waist high deep, and he took my hands.

At first I thought it was to steady me so I would not fall, but instead he pulled me close to him and kissed me gently on my lips.

He kissed me!

I had never been kissed before and I felt a surge of confused, excited emotions rushing through me, throwing me into a delirious state, tinged with fear as well. This was new territory for me.

I think I put my arms around his neck, and his arms went around my waist, but that was short-lived as the next thing I remember was him taking my hand again and shoving it down his swimsuit under the water.

I froze. I did not know what to do or what to expect. How in the world could I? I had never been that close to a man before and I was certainly still innocent. I had never been kissed or touched, let alone touched someone else, and this was a grown man.

I knew instinctively that this was wrong and wanted to leave immediately. My mind was telling me to run, but my body knew there was nowhere to go. Our friends had not yet returned.

In a sick twist of curiosity, I just stood there, my hand around his erect manhood.

He must have understood my shock, my untaught ways, and he decided to take advantage of this by proceeding to stroke himself with my hand.

I remember the feeling of the ridges, kind of bumpy and strange, and yet silky at the same time, while I also felt the pressure of his swim trunks against the back of my hand and the feeling of wet hair. I remember him making what sounded like a groaning sound and then he attempted to touch me, but I didn't let him.

After that, things are still a blur, but I recall hearing the sound of that boat returning to where we stood, that glorious sound that would save me from the awkward predicament I was in. At least this time.

We hung around with the other guy and his wife for a few hours after that, but if you asked me what we did or where we went, I couldn't tell you. I only remember an overwhelming feeling of guilt that came over me again and again, for the rest of that day and for many weeks to come, a guilt compounded by the fact that I couldn't tell anyone about what had happened, not my mother, certainly not my father, and even less my friends.

He was really cute, I had joined him in the sea, I had kissed him (or rather he had kissed me), and then I had held his erection in my hand and been forced to stroke it. I should have snatched my hand away; I should have screamed; I should have slapped him; I should have subjected him to a torrent of verbal abuse; I should have shamed him in front of his friends,

But I did none of these things. I left my fingers linger there – after all, I was curious and confused as well as shocked – and, yes, I didn't let him touch me, but I didn't do anything to ensure he never came near me ever again, to frighten him off forever.

And I could have done that. A more experienced girl, a girl who was more sure of herself might well have done that, and then all the pain of the next few years would probably never have happened. Eventually there would have been the wedding bells and the virginal white wedding dress my mother always said she wanted for me, and maybe a nice man and several children.

Yet, by doing nothing, by slinking away ashamed inside of myself, I unconsciously chose another path for my life, and as I write this, I am overcome with emotion.

I was not expecting these feelings, nor had I recalled to memory this event until I started writing it down.

As these memories are flooding my mind, and as I write them with tears flowing from my eyes, I feel angry. I am so upset at this moment, wishing I could jump into this scenario and drown him, or squeeze his balls until he screamed, or punch him, or run to the police. I am so disgusted and ashamed that I did none of these things, and I wish I could go into that scene again and save myself.

It wasn't fair! How could he have abused my trust and innocence this way? How could I have not stood up for myself? Sick! Sick! Sick!

It is true that, after that incident, we rarely went out to eat or socialize together, but we did occasionally. There was one night in particular that I remember when I agreed to let him take me to a dance out of town with my mom chaperoning us. It turned out to be a disastrous night as the car broke down on our way from home, but that's another story.

But why did I have anything to do with him at all? Why did I let him continue to insinuate his way into my life? Why did I forgive him even as I told myself I would never forgive or forget what he had done to me, how he had violated me, how he had had so little respect for me?

I suppose the answer is that he was cute and he had a good job, and so in some way I looked up to him and respected him. And he didn't immediately try anything further, so maybe now he respected me.

In hindsight, maybe I was much more confused and conflicted about the incident than I realized then or even understand now. For all the shame I felt, all the self-loathing, and all my loathing of him, I was also a pubescent girl whose curiosity about adulthood was growing beneath the surface somewhere in my subconscious.

My mother had taught me to protect myself, my reputation, and my purity. She always, always reminded me that, as a Catholic girl, I would be married in white. This is the generation I grew up in, the culture I grew up with, and a culture in which she was reared as well, one that was much more strict and demanding than you see today for sure. She was doing her very best for me and I hold no grudge against her, nor blame her for anything. I know she instilled in me what she knew to be best, under the standards taught to her by her mom and dad, and God.

Wait a minute … when I say, "I hold no grudge against her, nor blame her for anything," doesn't that indicate that, subconsciously, I may hold a grudge and may blame my mom for something? But how could that be? How could it have been her fault that a young, handsome boy thrust my hand down the front of his swimsuit when we were alone together and forced me to stroke him? What am I saying? What have I thought? Am I secretly blaming my mom for bringing me up too strictly so that I felt great shame at what happened, or am I blaming her for not being strict enough so as not to have prevented what happened to me? Maybe there is still a young teenage girl inside me who feels betrayed by being given the latitude to make my own mistakes.

Unfortunately, sometimes we don't learn unless we make mistakes and, in my case, many more were to come. It's what you learn from those mistakes, and how you can acknowledge God's hand in all of it, that really matters.

If you can look back and say to yourself, "I can't believe this or that happened," or "I can't believe I made that bad choice, but I see now the lesson taught, and I have learned from this by ...", then that is the real meaning to the error of our ways.

Can you look back on your tragedy or triumph and thank God for the many, many occasions you would have never made it through but for Him being there to get you past it?

My whole life I can now look back on and get the clear picture of how He was there to guide me, or protect me, or just see me through. I am so grateful.

Anyway, after a time X and I began to go out on "riding" dates, which mainly consisted of driving around the village in his car, usually at night. Crazily, inexplicably, I was disappointed that he never wanted to go to the beach or in the ocean with me after that first day. That is what I mean by me not really understanding then or now what was going through my mind. I was horrified by what he had forced me to do in the ocean, but at the same time I wanted him to take me back into the ocean because I loved the ocean (and was presumably prepared to take the risk).

Still, knowing the type of person he was, I am perplexed that he didn't insist on our returning to the scene of his crime. Here was a somewhat naïve young teenager willing to do anything for this guy, and who ended up doing just about everything for him, and yet he wouldn't take me to the beach.

It soon became apparent that X's intentions for these date rides were not merely for sightseeing, at least not of the gorgeous landscape that surrounded us. I eventually let my guard down and submitted to X taking full advantage of my innocence and naïveté so that our "date" rides eventually became lessons in making out. I say "lessons" because, as I mentioned earlier, I had never kissed or done anything with a man before him, so he cleverly, step-by-step, taught me everything he wanted me to know.

This is when my hell began.

It's amazing to me now, so many decades later, to look back on things and see how he was truly a predator, how he was grooming me and preparing me for the fall. But then I have to ask myself how much I was complicit in that. How much did I want to go where he was taking me, at least initially, without the guilt and shame of admitting to myself that I really, subconsciously, wanted to go there? People always say that there must have been something in it for victims of abuse to allow themselves to be exploited by a predator, and maybe, initially, there was for me too. It's just that I never wanted to sign up for the whole ride, for his whole agenda that I could never have conceived of at the time, and that I could never work my way out of as the noose tightened. It's that thing about the frog in ever-hotter water – it starts out feeling a bit disconcerting but not life-threatening and even pleasantly warm in its way – and then it burns you alive.

When we met, X said he was nineteen, and even at that he was much too old for me at that time. Later I would come to find out that he was really seven years older than me, not five.

I think it's important to mention that a five-to-seven year age difference is not a big deal when both parties in a couple are mature enough to be in a relationship. My parents are nine years apart and have been married over sixty years.

However, when you are a young girl of fourteen or fifteen, just beginning to try things and understand who you are and what you might want to become, a twenty-one-year-old man does not have any place in your life. This is a time when a young lady is trying to figure out how to be a lady and apply experiences in her life where every decision reflects her identity, her values and her name. Your reputation is the only thing that can follow you always, and it's a much easier load to carry if it is a good one.

We have a saying in Spanish that my mother would always quote to me, "Dime con quien andas, y te dire quien eres." This, literally translated, means, "Tell me who you are with, and I will tell you who you are."

When thought about romantically, men, boys – whatever they are at this age in a young woman's life – are just a mere distraction from school, friends and activities. I have often told my daughter that men in that way are for later on in life, to be figured out after the stress and chaos of adolescence, and school, or what to wear to the movies.

If you have friends who are male – great. Friends are so important in this stage of life, and I tell her that she can have as many friends as she wants, male and female, just nothing serious until she has had her education, her fun, her way of providing for her self-reliance and independence. Then she can invite another to share in those parts of her life too, if she wants to.

Chapter 5

Friendships

Because of where we lived, my friendships were very limited, and I mean *limited.*

I was twelve when we moved there and knew no one. As I previously mentioned, there wasn't an American school, just the local village grade school. My exposure to people consisted of the occasional trip to the bank, post office, grocery store or pharmacy, and walks on the beach.

On weekends people came from afar and spent a day at the beach. The main city was about an hour away and, in summer, dozens, and sometimes hundreds, of people would shatter our normally quiet and serene beach life with the sounds of music on their radios, of thumping their jet skis into the waves to see who could go highest, and of dogs barking. Occasionally a car or a truck would brave the sand and get stuck in it as it revved away trying to shake itself loose. The drivers would then turn to the police to pull them out, only to receive a ticket for driving illegally on the beach.

I remember the smell of hibachis grilling whatever was packed in people's coolers for the day, while the kids laughed and played in the warm, salty ocean water, building sand castles and having fun.

It was on one of these weekends that I met a girl named C. We spent most of an afternoon together on the beach and introduced our moms to each other. By the time the day was drawing to a close, we had become best friends. We exchanged mailing addresses and phone numbers, and vowed to stay in touch and to see each other as much as we could.

We did. It's what young girls do.

During those years, sleepovers and letters and good memories were shared. I remember one visit the family made back to the beach when C's mom invited me down there to eat tacos under the palm tree shacks, called "palapas," that were provided by the village for shade. It smelled wonderful, and she had fresh tortillas and salsa and all the trimmings for a good taco. The meat was tender and spicy, really good, and a little sweet.

After scarfing down a few of these delicious tacos, I asked her mom what her secret was as I had never tasted anything so good.

"Es conejo," she said.

What? "Conejo" is rabbit in Spanish, and needless to say I haven't eaten that since.

Our friendship was a good one for many years until X came along. Then slowly but surely we lost touch. It seemed as though the few friends I made or still communicated with from my childhood all eventually went away from my life completely once X came along.

Another friend I had made for a brief period in my life was a young American girl. Her family was from Tucson and she, too, came down for a few months out of the year with her parents. We didn't get along all that well, but at times we had fun. I believe she was about two years older than me, but we had each other to hang out with and entertain.

This went on for a while, until one day X said he had seen her on the side of the road, walking, so he had stopped to say hello. He claimed she flirted with him and threw a pack of condoms into the car, suggesting the obvious. He swore nothing happened with her, and to this day I have my doubts. Nevertheless, I took his side and she and I never spoke again.

Another good friend of mine from way back when, who was also a pen pal at first, was S. Her grandpa had a beach house in the village, and, as was customary, their family would make the five to six hour drive to stay a few days for the summer.

One afternoon, out of the blue, we got a knock on the door and it was S. I hadn't seen her in years. I was so glad to see her again to reminisce over our primary years. She looked so grown up as a teenager; same face but different body. I guess she thought the same of me too.

Unfortunately, when she came by, X was there and wasn't too happy that my time and attention were not on him. So he said he was going to leave.

I begged him to stay a little longer while I visited with my childhood friend.

He stayed and went to another room in the house but was upset, and that distracted me from enjoying her visit.

I ended up making a fool out of myself as I went from one room to the other and tried to divide myself and my time to appease both of my beloved guests. After all, they were both here to see me.

Eventually S asked me, "What the heck are you doing? If he wants to leave, let him. Does he have some hold over you or something?"

She unfortunately got frustrated and left, and I have never seen or heard from her again.

I'm sorry, S, for that stupid day. I wish I had seen then, through your eyes, the ridiculousness of my actions instead of wearing the blindfold that would remain over my eyes for years and years to come.

Before I met X, I had befriended a really nice man who worked for our village's street maintenance department. His name was J. He wasn't very well educated – in fact, he had not completed grade school – but he was a simple, humble man, and was always really nice to me and my parents.

In the evenings, he drove down our one main street and stopped at every light pole to switch on the night lamps. He drove a beige Dodge pickup with the village's logo on the door. We saw him occasionally at the Catholic Church in the village on Sundays, or as he drove by from time to time when I was walking my dog or taking out the trash. He eventually met a nice girl and became engaged, but he and I remained friends.

One evening I was saying hello to J in front of our home as he was turning on the street lights. He was sitting in the company pickup and I was standing next to it on the road. As we were chatting, my mom came out and greeted him as well. After a few minutes, mom told me dinner was almost done and to come in soon.

As we were wrapping things up, X drove down the road, probably on his way home. He passed us and suddenly stopped. With this, J respectfully drove off.

X started asking me all sorts of questions, visibly upset and acting jealous and crazy, such as, "What were you doing with him? What were you talking about with him? Is he your new boyfriend?"

He then informed me that I was not allowed to ever speak to J again, and that if I didn't obey his request, there would be consequences.

Of course, he did not state what those consequences would be, but I never spoke to my friend J again, at least not in X's presence. If I did see J in the village or passing by, it was a quick wave of the hand or a quick "Hola," but nothing more.

Looking back, I never really quite understood why X was acting that way and why he felt so threatened by another man, but it would later make sense to me.

Chapter 6

Gone forever

Shortly after this incident, X and I became more intimate, although I never went "all the way" with him, by which I mean that it never went all the way in, so what harm could be done?

After our rides, X and I would sit outside on the patio overlooking the ocean, and talk for a few hours with my mom, usually after sundown. On one particular evening we had gotten back from our ride and I was lying on the wall while my mom and X were each in a chair.

As I moved, mom noticed a blood stain on my white parachute shorts, which were very popular back in the 80s. She asked me if I had started my period, although I think, deep down, she knew what had really happened because she always kept tabs of when my monthly cycle was due. So I immediately went into the bathroom to check myself and clean up.

Mom was devastated, I was humiliated, and X ... well, he was scared.

Mom began to ask us all sorts of questions, which I don't remember other than, "What if you get pregnant?"

I remember her telling X he was to come to coffee the next morning so we could further discuss the matter at hand. I recall begging him to please show up the next day and not leave me stranded with this problem that he had gotten me into. I was so scared he wouldn't come.

Thankfully, he did show up the next morning, but I don't recall the conversation.

My mom then cried for three days straight although she said she would not tell Dad what had happened. I don't know where my dad was during this whole time; he was probably off working again. When bad things happened to me or I got hurt, Mom was usually alone.

I was fifteen.

I'm so sorry I hurt you, Mom, really I am. I love you.

Fortunately, nothing came of it as far as a pregnancy or STDs, but after some time of abstaining, things got heated up again when X rented a room from my parents and moved into my home.

I cannot imagine what my parents were thinking allowing this to happen. Here we were clearly experimenting with sex to the point that my mom was beside herself over it, and yet the next minute X's bedroom was literally across a corridor from mine.

The only bits I can remember about how X ended up living in our house, virtually on top of me, was that one day he didn't turn up for a scheduled visit, so my mom and I went round to his place to find him suffering from a crippling migraine. Then he and my dad came to a financial arrangement and X moved in. I don't think my dad had any idea about how sexually involved we were, but my mom did and must have decided to keep it from him and to go along with things.

I can't explain her reasoning and I cannot explain my role in what happened either because I simply cannot remember. Did I protest? Did I subconsciously want him living in our house? I certainly didn't scream the house down. I probably didn't kick up any fuss at all.

Maybe that is why my mom did not interfere. Maybe she thought it was what I secretly wanted and was prepared to indulge me whatever suffering it might cause her, and ultimately me,

X and I never hooked up in the actual house – we didn't sneak into each other's bedrooms to have full-on sex although we did make out – but as time went on we found many other places to get together and hook up for sessions that, from memory, only lasted five minutes at the most.

Between these hookups, we often argued or fought because I was very uncomfortable about what we were doing and only doing it to please him, and yet, at other times, things were really nice and loving between us.

I remember one day it was kind of cold outside and we had just gotten satellite TV. X had gotten trained in the States to sell and install these things, and had become the village's only supplier and dealer of this type of equipment. So business was good.

Back then, satellite TV broadcasting was free. All the premiums you now have to pay through the nose for didn't exist.

So on this brisk morning, X tuned into a popular music channel and we sat in a love seat all day watching videos while my mom worked in the kitchen, did house chores, went to the store.

I don't recall how long we were couch potatoes, but it was well into the afternoon. How selfish I was, but at the time how in love I was.

But soon it became apparent that this was to become my lifestyle for the next few years because X refused to involve me in his life outside of our house. If X's friends wanted to go somewhere, he would go. He water skied, and snorkeled, and rode the speed boats and jet skis, but hardly ever did he invite me to go along with him.

On one occasion, the couple who were there during the swimsuit incident were going to go out on their boat again. They invited X and told him to bring me along. Well, by then, X had bought a boat of his own, so we went on his boat instead and I did get to go this time. We rode the boat on the ocean from the village to the front of our beach house, but at that point X told me he was going to go drink and hang out with the guy and some other friends and I needed to leave. Being the avid ocean swimmer I was at the time, I didn't mind diving out of the boat and swimming to shore right in front of the house. I was about one hundred yards away, the water was warm and I could see through it, so off I went. That was fun. That ended up being a good memory, although there were not too many of those.

Around this time the business where X worked hired a temporary worker. She was older than I was and very pretty, and she had a terrible habit of flirting with X, especially when I was around. She made my life miserable for the few months she stayed working there.

One day, X came home from work for lunch with a bright red set of lip prints pressed to the back of his perfectly ironed white shirt.

As you can imagine, I flew into a jealous rage, demanding to know what the hell that meant and what was going on.

He insisted it was just a practical joke from his co-worker as she knew I was jealous and naïve.

This temp also made it a point to hitch a ride with X from her hotel to their work and back several times a week, as her hotel was conveniently between his work and home. On several of these occasions he would come home late, but he insisted they were just talking over a few drinks at the hotel bar about work and such.

This, of course, led to more fighting and more arguing between us.

My mother stepped in and told me to give him the benefit of the doubt and to trust him. So I did.

I spent many, many nights and afternoons doing so while tears poured down my face and my heart began to break.

I never knew what became of the temp. She eventually left and that was that.

Chapter 7

What is pornography?

X came home late one evening with a VHS tape in his hands and a really creepy smile on his face.

He seemed excited about the tape, so I asked him what it was. He hesitated at first, which irritated me and caused us to argue, then he confided in me that it was a "porno."

"A what?" I asked as I had never heard that word before.

He then explained what a porno was and I felt sick to my stomach.

"Why in the hell would you need to watch a sick thing like that, especially if you have me?" I demanded. "We are emotionally committed to each other, right? We are faithful and true to each other, and only each other, right? So what would you need this thing for?"

I made him swear he would not watch this filth by getting him to agree that this was not something he needed to see and therefore that he must promise that he wouldn't watch it, especially in my house.

He promised me he wouldn't. He swore to it. He agreed to it. And I trusted him, and again gave him the benefit of the doubt.

But that very same night I woke up because I had to use the bathroom, and as I stumbled into the hallway, I noticed a dim, bluish light coming out from the air vents in his bedroom.

It was about midnight and my immediate thought was, "No way! There is no way he is watching that porno. He swore!"

I quietly tried to open his door, but it was locked. I then squatted down to look through the vents to see if I could tell what was being watched, but his briefcase blocked all except about half an inch around the outside of the vents.

Damn!

I couldn't confront him without waking my parents. I couldn't make a spectacle because that was his space. He was paying for it. Was it even my place to say anything to him? We weren't married, but we might as well have been, right?

I was so confused and felt so betrayed, I went back to my room and cried. I can't begin to tell you how ashamed and embarrassed I felt. I recall quite clearly how raw and very real those feelings were. It was such a betrayal. It was so painful. He not only betrayed me and our relationship, but his word. He had promised, he had sworn he wouldn't view this filth.

I couldn't wait for it to be morning so I could confront him and finally catch him in a lie. I was ready to demand that he be thrown out of the house and call it quits.

Somehow in my naïveté and young years I knew his actions were wrong. I was confused and sickened about this whole thing. I wanted to slap him, and yell at him, and tell him to go to Hell. I wanted to feel his love and have him beg for me to forgive him and declare his dedication and faithfulness to me. After all, he owed me this after my sacrifice, after what I was prepared to do for him just to please him, didn't he?

I expected his abject contrition to come naturally. I had made the most treasured part of my body available to him, hadn't I? I had even given up going to the beach and to the water myself, just to be with him in the house.

I don't know, I was barely fifteen. I was trying to figure me out, trying to identify myself and who I was to become someday, who I wanted to be. How could he throw this wrench into our relationship by betraying me like that?

Morning didn't come soon enough. When I heard him open his bedroom door, I was ready. I confronted him right there between our two rooms and in horror asked him, "How could you? How could you lie and do it anyway?"

Of course he denied it at first and told me he did no such thing. He said he was just watching the news and regular TV.

So I asked him why he had to cover up the vents and lock the door if all he was doing was watching innocently.

He said it was to not disturb us with the light from the TV and that he locked the door so he wouldn't be disturbed.

Yeah, right!

By then my mom had come into the picture and demanded to know what was going on. I told her I wanted him gone, I wanted him to leave, to move out. That he had betrayed me, our relationship and his pledge.

I recall her saying there are two sides to any story, and although much of what occurred after that is fuzzy in my memory, I heard her say something that, if you knew my mom today, you would never believe she said, but she did.

She said that men watch these things because they need to. They watch these things so they can learn and know what to do when they get married.

I felt as though my heart sank. It felt as if X had just gotten away with it and wasn't going anywhere.

My next memory related to that event is an even more awful one. The details are unclear, but I went out somewhere and on my return I was headed toward the living room to watch TV when I saw a couple of chairs with a rope or string strewn across them, literally blocking the entrance to the room.

What is going on? I wondered as I saw X and my father in the living room, watching TV.

I thought to myself it must be an important football or baseball game. But no, that couldn't be as we used to always watch as a family the LA Dodgers play with Fernando Valenzuela at the pitcher's mound. That was good baseball.

Anyway, my mom told me not to go in there and I asked why.

She said, "They are watching that porno video X has, and you can't go in."

What? Are you kidding me? Betrayal all over again. And now, to add to the insult, my father was in on it as well? What was he thinking? How could he do this to my mom, to me?

When I was about six years old or so, I was playing hide and seek, probably with my mother at home.

In my generation you were not allowed in your parents' bedroom or in the living room without permission, so I hid in their bedroom closet, thinking this was a great place since I wasn't supposed to be in there anyway. Mom would never find me.

In the closet I came across a Playboy magazine, and having never seen such a thing, I opened it, much to my shock and surprise.

Scared and confused, I gave a shout out to my mom, who immediately came to my rescue, only to be shocked herself. Later on I was told theirs was a generation where Playboy magazine was read by men for the articles. It was a man's magazine and the wife at home had better mind her own business when it came to men's stuff.

What I don't know to this day is if she knew, prior to my discovery, that the magazine was there and was as truly shaken by the damn thing as I had been, or if she was simply playing along and reacting as I was hoping she would. That I'll never know.

What I do recall, though, is my parents burning it that night out in the enclosed trash barrel we had by the alley. I remember the darkness being lit up by the tiny sparks flying up into the air as that filth was being burned. To this day, I can see that image burned into my mind. Not the details, as I am sure I only looked at it for mere seconds, but I knew even then what pornography is. It destroys, it demeans, and it is filth.

Chapter 8

Survival

Not too long after this incident when I discovered X and my dad furtively watching a porno movie, our relationship became more toxic sexually, and somehow along the way X taught me to commit the act of fellatio on him.

I don't recall the first time I did it for him and I am certainly not proud of having done it. In fact, I am embarrassed to this day by the things I engaged in with him at such a young age just to keep him happy, to appease him. However, if this book is to help others who may be going through similar circumstances, especially in their teenage years, then it is worth revisiting and sharing the memories of my past.

Believe me, I am not bragging when I say I became very good at this act. Rather, I was forced to resort to it as a means of making him reconcile with me again. If we got into a quarrel or a fight, and I started to feel that he didn't love me anymore, no amount of cajoling on my part could get him to settle down. So, in time, I would give in, do this for him, and literally suck the anger out of him as he surrendered to the pleasure. When it was all over, when I had performed my part, it was usually all peaceful between us again as he was content to have got what he wanted out of me. Yes, 'content.' I wasn't expecting him to be happy; that would have been far beyond my reach.

Sometimes he would still be upset afterward, but his dark mood would be minimized by my illicit favors. The other stuff wasn't enough to bring him down to this mental state anymore. How could it when the average encounter was really just a five-minute quickie? As soon as he got himself off, we were done.

This went on many, many times. Kissing and hugging weren't really a part of our chemistry anymore, while fighting and arguing seemed to take their place to an ever-increasing extent.

Chapter 9

Black and blue

When I was about age sixteen, we were once again fighting about something – who knows what? – and it led to his bedroom, still at my house. I remember I could hear my mom cooking in the kitchen.

As we were in the middle of our heated discussion, I decided to leave, so I turned around and began walking away ... when it happened. For the very first time in my life ... it happened.

As I turned my back on him to literally walk away from the situation at hand, he punched me square in my back between my shoulder blades, knocking me down to the floor and onto my knees. I think it also knocked some of the wind out of me as I was going down.

The very next thing I remember is the feeling that he had betrayed me again. How could this person who said he loved me, to whom I had given my all, do this to me?

He had hit me!

As I began to get up, he almost immediately began to apologize and to swear over and over again that he didn't know what had come over him. He assured me repeatedly, and quite frantically, that he would never do it again, telling me how sorry he was and begging me to please forgive him He must have said this over half a dozen times.

I, again, was in a state of confusion, not sure which direction to take, an all too familiar feeling as when I discovered he had watched that porno tape at midnight.

What do I do now? This was a whole new experience for me.

So, you know what I did? Nothing. I forgave him. I believed him. I told no one. After all, it probably was my fault for turning my back on him as he was putting me down, right?

This began a pattern of lies, falsehoods and deceptions. I became the perfect pawn in his game.

You see, when you get hit and you say nothing, it gets easier for them. I made it easy for him to get away with it, with just about anything, from that point forward.

Oh, I didn't feel that was the case then. No, I only have understood that in the past decade or so, over thirty years later. When I look back on all the atrocities I later endured under his influence, it amazes me, because if I was then who I am today, there is no way they would ever have happened. I would have kicked him out long before he punched me, but I also would have told my parents immediately and they would have thrown him out, or worse.

But I didn't and those things had to happen for me to become who I am today. God has given me amazing strength throughout my life's journey.

What amazes me the most about it is that I didn't even know I had that God-given strength until after I went through it. I also drew strength from my mom's example of her endurance through some things best not to relate here.

Anyway, it got easier for him to demean me, to degrade me, and eventually to add emotional and verbal abuse to the physical assaults that frequently bruised my arms and my legs.

I would tell whoever asked whatever I could to cover it up and not to reveal my abuser or my weakness. After a while of drinking his twisted cocktail of abuse, I began to think it was all my fault. I hadn't expressed myself correctly or I hadn't done something right. If I had only kept my mouth shut or not spoken out of place. *He will change, though,* I told myself. *He will see he is making a mistake or I can change him.*

And during this time, I am wondering in my naïve teenage mind, W*hy? Why is he treating me like this when I gave him me? I gave him everything I had to give.*

In time, the words became equally as harsh as the blows. Yet another one of those moments of 'if I knew then what I know now,' but so true! That old cliché rings very true to those of us who can apply it to our own circumstances, doesn't it?

I was a very attractive young lady in my budding years of adolescence, just trying to figure me out. I had dreams of becoming a model someday, or of starring in a TV show or commercial.

In fact, I had a small cameo appearance the year prior to meeting X. I had been cast in a commercial for a clothing store in the main city. They came and brought the camera crew to our village, to my home, and cast me there, right at my beach house.

It was so much fun. In fact, one of the boys on the set had even met Chuck Norris in a skit he had done for a martial arts product or school in the same city. At any rate, I enjoyed it.

I also had aspirations of becoming a criminal prosecutor. That I owe to my mom and all the detective and lawyer shows she watched when I was little, shows like 'Perry Mason,' 'Ironside.' 'Murder, She Wrote.' and 'Judge Judy' (I love 'Judge Judy.' I still watch her from time to time. Go, Judy!)

In time X convinced me that I would never amount to anything. He loved using profanity. He used to say, "You have no talent," or "Every woman wants to be a model, or famous, and all they become are whores."

He also would tell me I smelled bad and that I was ridiculous, uneducated and stupid. Many of these put-downs were also accompanied by him hitting me.

He always found a way to make it feel like it was my fault and that none of this would be happening if it wasn't because of me. And I eventually came to believe it all.

Conversely, there were times – albeit few and far between – when he was the epitome of sweetness, and even became romantic. On good days he would call me beautiful. He would hold my hand sometimes when we watched TV. There aren't many memories of these precious moments, though, so there is no need to expand on this point.

Needless to say, time went on and things only worsened. One time we went to the main city for groceries and other errands. For whatever reason, we got into an argument. It became physical, and as we were driving back home in his car, which, at this time was a VW Rabbit Sport Edition, he just reached over and hit me on the face and head. He was yelling at me to shut up and many other vile and profane things.

All I recall at this time is the hitting and him swerving the car as he did so.

I remember a car passing and looking in, but the occupants did nothing. I was crying, desperate, and bewildered at this abrupt display of violence toward me in such a small, confined space. I felt very confused at what had just happened to me, and yet again couldn't understand why. I felt betrayed and even afraid.

By the time we got home, after about an hour's trip back, it was as if nothing had happened.

That is all I remember of that day.

Chapter 10

Eleven

On another occasion, we again got into some stupid argument that got physical, and I remember feeling so disheartened by then. I was also getting more fearful of him, but no way was I going to show him that. I had already begun to believe his verbal attacks on my self-esteem and self-worth. I vividly recall we had been intimate eleven times by this point.

After the fight, I ran to the backyard of our house. I don't know if he drove off or went in the house. Either way, I was alone outside, crying and feeling so isolated and desperate. Despair set in. I was confused and hurt and ashamed. I felt worthless and dirty, and that this was all my fault.

I remember squatting up against the brick wall, the bricks still warm from the afternoon sun, and looking across the way at my mom's cherry tomato plants. I don't like tomatoes, but they were so pretty and ripe and ready for picking. I remember looking at the silly tomatoes and feeling how lucky they were to be growing freely and being taken care of ever so gently, and in turn providing us with a lovely harvest. I really do recall feeling sad at the simplicity of their beauty compared to the miserable situation I was in.

As huge teardrops ran down my face, I took a sharp rock, and amidst my surge of emotions, I began to carve the number eleven on my upper thigh. I wanted to permanently embed into my skin the number of times I had done this filth with him and therefore punish myself for it. This is how I reasoned the pain away in order to cope.

Fortunately for me, although it hurt and it did leave the eleven on my skin for a few days, it did not permanently scar me. I am very thankful for that.

The incredible thing is that you really begin to lose feeling, both emotionally and physically, when you are in this state of mind and emotion.

Chapter 11

His way or the highway

There were so many different things that took place after that, little things that would cause me heartache or doubt. Things like him going out with his friends and having fun, but not taking me along. Him staying out late or all night, then getting home without an explanation, and when I insisted on one, we would end up in a quarrel or a fight.

On one of these nights I recall him getting ready to leave for a second time. It was late and I was upset at him going somewhere again without me and not telling me where or with whom he was going.

He had bought a truck by now, and it was tall with big mud tires and visible suspension. I had to grab the door handles just to get in. As he was getting ready to back out of our driveway, I was standing between the open driver's door and the seat and we were arguing.

I don't recall his exact words, but they were pretty much the same by now: put downs and insults, usually.

I was crying and demanding an explanation, when he suddenly put the truck in reverse. It caused me to step back, but my arm was still caught in the door as he tried to shut it on me.

He stopped the truck from moving, but the engine was still running and he continued to attempt to shut the door on my left arm.

Now, remember, the truck was high, so the distance from where he was sitting to where I was standing was at quite an angle. Not only did it hurt my forearm, but my shoulder as well. My whole arm started to feel bruised and very sore.

I was still crying, and must have been doing so loudly because my mother came outside to ask what was going on. X told her I was preventing him from leaving and embellished the situation far beyond what had really happened.

The next thing I recall is Mom pulling me away from the truck and trying to settle me down. Her words were a fog as I watched him back out the rest of the way and leave in a fit of rage.

Idiot!

But me or him? He really hurt me emotionally and physically that night. You want to talk about desperation and despair? Feeling like there really will never be a way out?

On yet another occasion I decided to walk from my house to the village's main hotel about two miles away. This hotel sits at the crest of the hills as you begin to drive downhill. I had walked this far because I had had it with X! I was tired of my circumstances and my secret life. We had certainly gotten into another stupid fight and I was done. So I just took off.

It wasn't unusual for me to go for very long walks on the beach, so I probably told my parents that's where I was going, if I even told them at all. I cannot recall.

At that time, and in my state of emotional distress, tired and abused in mind, body and spirit, I concocted the idea that I would simply lie down in the middle of the road just past the hotel and wait for X to run me over.

He wouldn't be able to see me as he drove his huge truck over the crest of this hill, and as physics would prove, the downhill slope would prevent him from seeing me lying in the road.

I knew more or less about what time he would be driving home, so it should all work out just fine. In my mind it would soon be over. All my pain, all my humiliation, and all my faults and bad decisions would be taken care of.

So I lay down on the asphalt and waited.

I was scared, but as I mentioned before, the incredible thing is that you really begin to lose feeling, both emotionally and physically, when you are in this state of mind and emotion. Can you relate?

Somehow, no one drove over the hill at that moment.

I don't know how long I lay there or how I got up and out of there. It's a blur to this day, but I remember X holding me and comforting me as I cried. Obviously I survived it and didn't get hurt, at least not physically, and not during that encounter. I believe this was yet another time that God was watching over me.

I still had the mental torment and had to deal with the emotional aftermath of such a decision, but somehow I got past it.

Chapter 12

A taste of freedom

About this time, my dad had to go down south from where we used to live for several months to work.

By now he had changed jobs, but we did not move again. Instead he rented a quaint, yet practical, apartment where he traveled for a few months of the year to do this work.

He thought it would be a good idea for me to try and learn some skills with him, and so I went down with him for about a month. I was seventeen, almost eighteen.

I was excited and scared at the same time as I had no idea what to expect. By this time X had brainwashed me so much that, even though I would have the wonderful opportunity to reunite with some of my childhood friends, I was afraid they would no longer accept me.

I also was under a strict schedule as far as X was concerned. I had to be there *if* he called. I had to be there *if* he checked in on me. What if he called and I was out with my friends? He would be upset. Besides, what business would I have to be out anyway, right? He was all I needed, he was the only person I reported to, loved, and wanted to be with.

I remember my friend P called to invite me to go with him and a bunch of others – some of whom I knew and others I didn't – to dinner and a movie. I wanted to see them all and go with them so much, but I didn't go.

On another night, another friend called and said there was a party at a mutual friend's house. This was also in the neighborhood where we used to live and right next door to P's house. This one I was not about to miss, so I asked my dad for permission to go, and he said yes.

Oh, it was so good to see the old friends from the block. I had had a crush on one of them when I lived there. He was very cute. He was half Italian and half Spanish. Tall, green eyes and naturally tan skin. He had a dream to become a professional soccer player, and when we lived there, he was going down that path very successfully.

He was there that night because the party was at his parents' house. It was so good to see him and he still looked good. No, actually, he looked really hot. He was now about nineteen or twenty, not twelve or thirteen, which is how old he was the last time I saw him.

We all had a good time catching up and laughing. We flirted a little and had a few shots of tequila, along with some delicious dip and chips someone had made.

I remember feeling a little buzzed for the first time ever in my life, but nothing too serious. It was fun, it was daring, and it was different.

The night began to unwind, and I had to get back to the apartment. P, who had picked me up from the apartment, loaned his car to our other friend, who drove me home.

I remember feeling so nervous and excited at the same time. Here I was with my puppy-love crush, sitting next to him in the front seat as he drove through the city.

I wanted to rewind the time and pretend the night had just started and that I did not have a boyfriend back home. I wanted to spend more time with this gorgeous young man and get to know him better

But fate was not having it.

When we arrived back at the apartment, way too soon, and as I nervously began to turn to open the door, he nervously reached over and gently took my chin and turned my face to his. I was not going to pass this up as I knew I would never see him again.

He gently kissed my lips and made a comment similar to "Quisas en otra vida," meaning "Maybe in another life."

He opened my door, walked me up to the apartment, and hugged me goodbye. It was such a different and welcoming experience to be treated with respect and dignity. We broke our embrace and I opened the door to the apartment.

I looked out the window as he got back into our friend's car and drove away.

Many years later, I would have the opportunity to return to this city and revisit all my friends. Much to my surprise, I saw this young man again. He had gotten a little chubby – not too much – but was still very handsome. I noticed a sadness in his eyes, almost a look of defeat.

A little later we were able to say hello to one another, and as we were catching up, a thin, dolled-up, too much make-up and fake nails, too many trips to the tanning salon, woman came up to him and told him he needed to do something.

He left, and as he walked away I looked over at P with a "Who's that?" expression. He came over and told me she was our friend's wife. He had gotten her pregnant and forsook his soccer career to do the right thing. He was now selling gold jewelry as a means of income, one which she lavishly advertised quite flamboyantly in her own accessorizing.

It saddened me to see his potential go right down the drain, and yet I realized he was the one who got himself into that situation. I kept my distance after that. I never really knew what happened to him after that night.

I had tears in my eyes when I came back from the party. My dad was already in bed and asked me if I had had a good time.

I said, "Yes," and although I was still feeling a little buzzed, was grateful he did not call me into his bedroom for I feared I probably smelled of tequila.

I got ready for bed, said my prayers, and laid my head down on the pillow. My head was spinning, but the memories of that evening lulled me to sleep.

The next day, I asked my dad if X had called and I think he said no. I don't recall, but it didn't matter. For one night, even though X was constantly on my mind, I got to be a girl – a happy, flirty young girl.

I don't know when this night took place in the timeline of my month's stay with my dad. I do recall getting several phone calls and invitations to various things which I turned down. I wish now I had gone to every single one of them and instead created lifetime memories alongside friends who cared about me, had my back, and wanted me to be around them. Oh, how I wished for many years that I could have erased all those times I said no and just lived, but the influence and control X had over me, the fear he had so vividly instilled in me, could neither be replaced nor taken away.

Chapter 13

The proposal

Ironically, back at home, Mom was planning a trip down to meet us. The three of us would then drive back home, which was about a twenty-four-hour drive.

I don't recall if she had already arrived or if she was still home and getting ready to leave, but X got himself into trouble.

X had a friend – I'll call him F – who was married, and his wife (whom I'll call L) and I inevitably became friends. She, too, had been slapped around like me, so we shared that in common, but not too much more. Sad, isn't it?

We had girl talk and occasionally we would compare our partners to each other. Then we would laugh and cry. We ended up hanging out quite a bit together.

I was still seventeen.

Well, one day, X called, panicked and hysterical. He said his friend was threatening to kill him and that he had to leave the area immediately.

While we were away, X had moved in another friend, T, from his hometown, to stay for a few weeks. That's another story, but that dude was weird. He had his own issues. Anyway, F allegedly caught L and X having sex in his bed at our home. That is the story X told us, while insisting that F was fabricating the whole thing. When all of us – my dad, my mom, and especially me – asked X for more details, he insisted that nothing had happened between him and L, and it was all just a huge misunderstanding.

When I asked T, X's childhood friend, he was as useless and clueless as the next guy, so he served us no purpose.

X kept insisting he was innocent but was packing his things, ready to leave for the USA, when somehow I convinced him to wait for us to get back home, which was in a few more days.

He agreed to wait, but on condition that we got married and left for the USA as soon as possible.

Was he proposing to me? Over the phone?

Here I was, hundreds of miles away, not able to see his face when he proposed to me or when he frantically explained the events leading up to this mess.

By then I had gotten really good at giving him the benefit of the doubt that my mom had taught me to do so well a few years before.

I screamed, "Of course we'll get married as soon as we can. But don't leave! Promise you won't leave before we get home. Swear it!"

He did and waited for us to return.

Now that I was engaged, a friend of mine took me to a huge mall there in that big city. I had never seen anything so large in my life, so many stores, so much variety. It felt intense.

She took me to an intimate wear store and told me to come check out these strange looking panties, something I had never seen or heard of before in my life. As she showed me some of these fascinating remnants of clothing, I recall a certain pair capturing my full attention. They were a leopard print with black lace all around the edging. They were very silky and soft, but they weren't finished.

As they sat there neatly folded on the table along with several other styles and colors, I pulled them up and said to her, "Look, they didn't finish making these."

She chuckled at me and said, "That's the way they are made. They are supposed to be like that. It's called a thong."

We laughed, and after I figured out how they were to be worn, I felt a little naughty at the thought of how this thong was going to look on me someday after I was a married woman, so I purchased them.

They were wrapped ever so delicately in tissue and placed in a fancy, glossy paper bag that sported the lingerie shop's name. And off we went to explore the rest of this expanse she called a mall.

After we returned to the apartment, I took this piece of clothing, my secret garment, and hid it deep in my suitcase. It was to stay hidden until a special night where it could be properly sported and best displayed on my trim, young, and sexy body.

"Someday soon," I thought.

A few days later, we proceeded to head back home.

I was now turning eighteen.

Chapter 14

Conditions of consent

My father had given his consent to our marriage with the condition that I attend college and get a degree. He insisted on this, and X promised he would put me through school. My long-lost dream to be a criminal prosecutor was soon a thing of the past, but, as promised to my father, I would attend a semester of college with plans to pursue a Bachelor's Degree in Business Administration.

I had been homeschooled for the previous few years and simply got tired of it. Between the distractions of the beach, a boyfriend, and the hidden life of abuse, torment, and sex, I could no longer concentrate on finishing high school.

We planned on moving to the USA to live and work with my uncle, who had his own business and housing on the property. We would all go up and visit him. Then I would go to the local university and apply for my G.E.D. But first we would take a mini family vacation to Disneyland. Along the way, we would also visit some old friends my parents knew in California. We stayed with them for a couple of days on our way through.

I vividly remember this because, on our first morning there, we were awakened by a small rumbling noise and rocking of the floor. As I sat up, I saw the small chandelier above the dining table swaying back and forth ever so gently. I was terrified. R, my dad's friend, said we had just had an earthquake and it was no big deal.

No big deal? I had never felt anything like it in my life. A few aftershocks followed, but soon it became apparent that these minor tremors were almost a daily thing in this part of California.

No, thank you! You can keep those earthquakes to yourself, California.

Later that evening, we were all supposed to go eat dinner at some fancy restaurant they liked, and it would be their treat. As I was getting ready to go, I remember putting on a little lipstick, combing my hair, and putting my lip-gloss into my purse, when at the last minute X said he didn't want to go.

I thought, 'How rude! We can't do this to them.'

I expressed my opinion to him but he did not agree and did not appreciate hearing my comments on the matter.

They were expecting us and we had already said yes; in fact, I think they had even made reservations.

Now, what would *you* do? You would probably say something like, "Fine, then, stay here all alone. I'm going."

Right?

I sure would have said that today if faced with the same situation, but instead I gave in. I did so because that is not how it works if you are in a domestic violence relationship. That is not what you can say.

What you say is what I said to my parents and hosts. "We're staying here. X doesn't want to go."

Even my mom tried to encourage me to go with them and I said no. I think X felt inadequate compared to the rest of the group, that they were too good for him. So we stayed and they went on to have a wonderful dinner.

We ended up fighting, which later led to some sort of sexual experience (obviously nothing too memorable). Remember, this was not a pleasurable moment shared between two lovers who had respect for one another. This had become a way to make him content. It had become a form of self-preservation for me, a sort of subconscious protection of myself.

Afterward, I went outside for a long time, walking around the garden and looking at the flowers. I felt so alone, ashamed and embarrassed at what had become of me and my life.

I don't know what X was doing while I was outside.

A short time after that, my parents and their friends returned and shared with us that they went sightseeing and visited a famous wax museum which was something I really wanted to see. To this day, I have not had the opportunity to go back and do so.

Maybe someday.

Chapter 15

Control

Looking back on that afternoon, I see how controlling X was. Believe me, abusers gain power and dominion over you and you lose your agency. You feel as though you no longer have choices. You become a mere puppet or pawn in their game.

But if you are involved in an abusive relationship, stop! And I am telling you there is hope. I promise you there is. How else would I be writing my experiences now if there hadn't been hope, a way out?

You have to want to get out and you somehow have to try to remember who you are, who you still are deep inside. Reconnect with yourself, your spirit.

Listen to me, I understand, I really do, for I am you and you are me.

I told no one. I thought I had no one to help me or to listen to me because I did not let anyone in. It was too shameful, too humiliating. I know about the grasp, the hold he has on you. It can be broken, trust me. Be of good courage and know your worth. You have value. It is not your fault, whatever "it" is. There is hope. Please open your mind and pray about your way out as you continue to read my experiences, my memories, and my moments of despair.

I share these with you from the bottom of my heart in order to touch you, to touch your soul.

Don't give up. Please don't give up.

You can do this. You are wonderful.

You are beautiful, and, most of all, you are worth it!

Well, we went to see my uncle and made the arrangements with the university nearby for me to take my G.E.D. We also talked to my uncle about living there and X working for him while I attended school after we were to be married.

We stayed a few days, visiting and enjoying each other's company. Then, one afternoon, while X was getting upset about something, he and I began to quarrel.

Before it could escalate, I invited him down to the basement where there was a bedroom, living room, and TV.

I can't remember if X was staying there during our visit or not, but someone in our family was sleeping down there.

We turned on a popular music channel and a Madonna song came on. I didn't want to argue anymore and just wanted him to be calm, so I convinced him to have sex with me.

He really didn't want to at first, but I insisted, and after a while he gave in.

I still remember the song playing as I lay underneath him on that basement couch. I remember feeling a glimpse of hope that maybe, after we were married, things could change and be more like this moment. Maybe he would love me and treat me better after we exchanged vows.

So I silently cried to myself as he did his thing, without protection, and then left me there to clean up.

What harm could come of it anyway? We would be married in just a few weeks. What was the big deal?

We must have gone back home to Mexico for a little while, I guess to gather our things, because the very next thing I remember is coming back to the States and getting married in the town's courthouse in front of the Justice of the Peace. I was barely eighteen and he had just turned twenty-five.

By now the fact that he had lied about his age at the beginning didn't matter because we had been together for three years and too many things had happened between us. He was my first and only in everything, and he was the one I was going to marry, no matter what. I knew he would change once the marriage took place and that all would be well. I just knew it!

We signed the marriage license and were legally husband and wife. I think my parents were the witnesses, and my aunt and uncle threw us a quaint little dinner to celebrate. I can't recall if there were any gifts exchanged at that time. I just remember beaming and feeling hope that this would be a new and grand beginning and experience for us.

We still needed to be married in church, and to do so we had to attend a six-month course of couples' counselling.

I was all for it. He was not.

Chapter 16

Darkness and betrayal

A few days after we were married by the JP, we decided to go to the big city a few hours away on a little getaway for just a couple of days – a sort of mini honeymoon you might think – but that was far from the real reason.

After we had spent the afternoon on that basement couch, I got pregnant. I didn't know right away and can't recall when exactly I found out. I just remember missing my period and panicking.

I had to have found out sometime right before we were married, because the trip to Phoenix was to terminate the pregnancy. The doctor, who was the family doctor at the time, had checked me and given me all the information we needed, where to go, and what to do.

I was so scared and confused, but knew that if I told my parents about the pregnancy, I would bring shame to the family, and that could not happen. You see, I had already broken my mom's heart when I was fifteen when she discovered what we had done by the blood on my white shorts. She had raised me to be a modest and decent girl who would marry in white, no matter what.

I remember feeling fear and regret on the way to the clinic, trying to figure out options or a way to tell, a way to scream out loud the despair and hopelessness I was feeling at that moment.

When we arrived at the clinic, I wanted to use a fake name and lie so no one could ever know. I remember having to fill out some papers. I don't know now what they were, but I know that I used my real name. I couldn't change it. Despite all I had done and had become, an honest and a good person still was in me. Somewhere inside, broken and battered, she was there.

After a while, they called me into the back room, where a nurse laid me down on a cold steel table and was very nice to me. A thin paper sheet separated me from that hard cold table as she got me ready. She was professional, but I could tell she felt sorry for me.

A couple minutes later, the doctor came in and stood next to me as the nurse gave me a sedative. He asked her if I was ready and said, "OK, let's begin."

He said nothing to me as he began the horrible procedure, one that would become my prison for the rest of my life.

A thin sheet lay over me. The procedure hurt. It felt like a horrible period with bad cramps. He told me to hold still and it wouldn't be much longer as the nurse held my hand. I was crying inside, a part of me dying, and there was nothing I could do. I just wanted to get out of there and run as fast and as hard as I could.

Soon the doctor shook me awake and said it was over and that I needed to sit up and go relax for a little while in another room while another desperate young girl came in for the same thing.

As he was getting ready to leave, I asked the doctor about how far along I had been and he said it was about a month.

The nurse helped me get down off this sacrificial altar and also helped me get my clothes back on, and then escorted me to a waiting area where I was to relax.

I faintly recall other girls in this room, all of us sitting there surrounded by what appeared to be scattered pre- and post-abortion pamphlets and other reading materials. Were they feeling the same horror as I was? Were they also heartbroken and lost? The whole thing immediately after is such a blur to this day.

I was tired, devastated, sore, and terrified of what had just happened. I wanted to get back to our cheap motel, and just be held and comforted by my new husband. We had only been married a few days and all I wanted was his love and support at this horrible time. I needed an escape of sorts, somehow a word, a gesture justification that what had just happened somehow was OK.

What I got was nothing less than horrific.

What was supposed to be a bonding time by two mourning parents soon turned out to be a horrible fight. As I lay in the motel in a fetal position, waiting for X to come out of the bathroom, I was crying and desperate for comfort. When he finally came out, I asked him, begged him, to come lay with me and just hold me, to comfort me with a silent embrace.

He hesitated, and although I cannot recall his words, they were harsh and mean, as usual. Then he yelled at me, cussing me out with all sorts of colorful expletives.

As I approached him to put my arms around him, he slapped me and pushed me up against the motel wall next to the bed I had been lying on.

He hit me! I had just gone through a horrific physical and emotional trauma, and he hit me! Yes, he hit me.

At that moment I wanted to die. At that moment, something bad became tragic reality for me. This was to be my reality for the rest of my life. Now I could never get out, not after this. Here he was betraying me, betraying my trust once again like he had before.

My heart sank to a new low, one that I believe broke it, and for a long, long time would not be mended.

After he hit me and pushed me against the wall, I don't know what happened. I draw a blank. I don't remember anything after that. Maybe my mind has blocked it out, as it has so many other experiences.

At some point, we made it back home and life as a married couple began.

I can only imagine that, while on that trip, we must have promised to never speak about it to anyone, ever. A secret bonding us together forever began, an inescapable prison became my household, and a horrible life began to unfold.

Chapter 17

A new chapter

I received my G.E.D. and was now enrolled at the local university, and just as we had promised my father, I began courses toward a Bachelor's in Business degree.

It was a very difficult transition for me to go from homeschooling back to the public school system. I struggled adapting to such a large environment, trying to understand credits, and parking permits, and what to wear.

I don't recall whatsoever what our means of income was other than X helping my uncle at his business. I shopped at the local Goodwill store for my new school attire as I had no concept of fashion or what was in or not. I didn't grow up that way. Growing up, we were humble in means and money and didn't have a lot, but we had what we needed.

This now was a foreign environment to me in every sense of the word: A new country, a new school, a new society and its expectations, a new everything. I felt so lost and alone.

I persevered and signed up for accounting, CIS, and business law. I did OK in these, except accounting. At the end of the first semester, I failed that class (I had never gotten an F before in anything), and I never went back.

I started helping out at my uncle's store just a little, to avoid boredom more than anything, and, in exchange, we lived rent free in a small apartment on the property. At least I think it was rent free. X managed all the money and I never really saw any of it.

Things got worse between me and X, and some days were really, really bad.

On one particular evening, after X had worked all day, he came home and took a shower. I decided it was a good time for a romantic evening, so I set out a large blanket on the living room floor next to the non-functional fireplace. I placed a candle in the fireplace instead, turned to some soft music on the small stereo that was provided, and put on a skimpy baby doll top and that sexy leopard print thong I had bought at the mall. I had never worn it, and tonight was the night!

As I heard him turn off the water to the shower, I dimmed the lights, lay on the blanket, and positioned myself in a sexy pose. Not a provocative one per se, but a modest one. I made sure some of the thong was showing while leaving plenty for the imagination.

I was excited. We had never really had a night like this before, so I was looking forward to it.

As he came out of the shower and asked where I was, I sheepishly said to him, "Come to the living room and find me." My heart was racing as I expected him to lie next to me and ravish my body. I saw him walk to the doorway that separated the bedroom from the living room, just wearing a wet towel around his waist. "Here it comes," I thought. "He is going to love this!"

After all, what man wouldn't? I was young and taut and very pretty. I was ready to explore new things that I had every right to explore as a new and curious bride.

As he came closer to where I was, he looked at me and said, "What the hell are you doing?" and then chuckled a little, adding, "Get off the floor. You look like a cheap whore!"

He turned around and went to get dressed while I felt humiliated and ashamed. I don't remember what happened the rest of that night.

There were so many times during this period that we had physical altercations, almost always accompanied by verbal and emotional abuse.

Instead of going into detail on every single incident, I am going to mention some of them briefly as I move on to the next period in our married life, where things just were not getting better and actually took another turn for the worse.

One day X broke my grandma's antique mirror off her dresser and then proceeded to grab some of the broken glass and stuff it down my shirt. I instinctively reached in to pull the glass out and deeply cut my finger in the process. I still have that scar and X got the bill. The mirror had a beveled edge and he had to pay to replace it so my uncle wouldn't notice.

Another time we were arguing, and as he went to kick me one more time, I placed my hand in the way of his kick, causing the bone in the top of my hand to be pushed up and to snap like a toothpick. We went to the doctor and told him the door had slammed on my finger during a gust of wind.

Another time we had a fight in my uncle's store – fortunately there were no customers at the time – and I, for the first time, cussed him out. In retaliation, he chased me throughout the store to the back of the house, where he punched me. All I can remember after that was seeing stars and blacking out.

Another time we were fighting and he kicked me to the ground and began dragging me by the hair, causing painful welts on my head. I could feel the hair start to detach from my scalp.

I straightened my long fingernails and thought, "If this is it, then I'm taking some of him with me!"

So, as I lay on the ground, I reached up and dug my fingers into his thigh as deep as I could. Then everything went dark.

Like I said, there were many too many moments of abuse; too many even to recount.

Does any of this sound familiar to you? Maybe not the exact physical abuse, but perhaps the control, the humiliation and the hopelessness? The patterns they follow are all the same.

Well, life was not getting any better and I stopped coming out of the apartment altogether. I stopped talking to my aunt and rarely saw my uncle. I would contact my parents long-distance several times a month and never said a word about what was happening.

Why? Because I felt shame, fear and despair. I had a terrible secret to keep and knew, just knew, that if I left him, he would tell. After all, he always reassured me that if I ever called the cops on him and he was arrested, I would not live to see the rest of the day when he got out. Also, if he could do this to someone he claimed to love, and took vows before God and witnesses to proclaim it, and then turned around and hurt me in this way, what was he capable of doing to my family?

My parents were older and had no idea what was happening to their daughter, their only child. I had to protect them.

This was truly my thought process then and for so many years to follow.

Chapter 18

Escalating violence

One day he beat me so bad that he turned his rage to my face. I still can feel the wedding ring on his finger hitting against my lips and teeth, causing severe bruising on both the inside and the outside of my mouth, as well as around my eye.

Then he took pictures. The son of a bitch took pictures of my bloody, swollen mouth and said I looked like a boxer.

He actually had the film developed and I do not understand how that was even possible without the authorities being notified. Maybe the photo shop did notify them – I will never know – but during this time domestic violence was not yet a felony, and when it became one, it was just a little too late for me.

But, as you know, when you are in the middle of this torture, you cannot report it. You must hide it and take all precautionary measures to protect the abuser and to never let anyone know of the abuse.

You can never escape.

Well, he picked up the pictures and thumbed through them. When the ones of the abuse came up, he chuckled and threw them at me to see.

Once again I felt so humiliated, so lost and alone. He then simply ripped them up and threw them away.

From that moment on, I began begging God to help me die in my sleep, to take me home, away from all this misery. I kept asking but nothing was happening. Had God abandoned me too?

After all, this was my fault, right? X would always remind me of this, especially during a fight. Or he would tell me how useless, ugly or worthless I really was.

I even started holding my breath at night, hoping I could stop breathing, at the same time in my mind silently screaming at how devastating this would be to my parents, especially to my mom, who had waited fifteen years to finally have me. How could I do that to her?

I prayed and continued to beg God for a way out, but it wouldn't come for another few years. How was I to know?

Then, one day, when my aunt and uncle were out of town, X decided we would pack up everything and move out at night, and go live in a local rundown motel room.

I hated the idea. It wasn't fair to my family to just run off without notice and without an explanation. It went against everything I knew to be right, but he didn't care.

So, on the night before we knew my aunt and uncle would be coming home, we left.

X had gotten an idea that he would buy out a business he was interested in from a local man and then buy us a house, which he then proceeded to do. I don't know how he managed it; I think he may have borrowed money from my dad, but I don't recall. At any rate, he did buy the business and he did buy us a house not too far from that business.

The business began in a small office space and later grew to be a large and seemingly successful one as the only dealer authorized to carry out repairs of its kind in our town.

It was at this point that I lost all interest in working for X and just stayed home. He was very upset about that decision.

One day, I stopped in at the office where he had three or four employees working in the back. We got into a fight in his office and he slapped me, pulled me by the hair, tossed me around, and threw me over his desk onto the floor.

One of the guys, a big guy whose name I can't recall now who had always been nice to me, came over and asked him what the hell was going on, and it was made very clear to him that he needed to mind his own business or he would be out of a job.

He, unfortunately for me, just looked at me with despair in his eyes and walked away.

Humiliated yet again, I picked myself up from the office floor and took my battered and bruised body back home.

When I got home, I thought it would be a good idea to take a warm shower to help ease the pain I was feeling both physically and emotionally. As I entered into the soothing water of my shower, my head really hurt. I massaged it and began to shampoo my hair. Then, all of a sudden, globs of hair started to come out.

I freaked out and got very scared. I had the most beautiful full head of hair, so what was going on?

As I continued to rinse, I felt the bumps on my scalp where once again my hair had become detached. I began to cry quite hysterically as I realized why it was falling out like that.

After I got out of the shower, I was able to get a comb through my wet hair, and although it hurt my head to do so, I continued to comb it until all the loose hair was gone.

I could go on and on telling story after lurid story of such events, similar or worse to the many I have already described, as I sit here pondering on what to write next, and wondering if it is necessary to continue in such detail.

Years went by, the violence got worse, betrayals became frequent, and threats were common. There were constant random fits of rage and anger.

I didn't have freedom or control over many decisions. I asked for money to go to the grocery store or for a new outfit. I never ever saw the checkbook, yet there was always cash in his wallet which I was not allowed to touch without permission.

Broken eggs flying through the house after a grocery store stop; or a ketchup bottle broken against the living room wall, making it look like a murder scene; or potted plants strewn all over the carpet and me being forced to clean up the mess. These were all becoming a part of my life, just because he was mad about something ... about nothing.

A full beer can thrown at my back while I was walking away in front of his family and friends didn't seem to matter to anyone, or the childhood baton I once used in a school parade broken across my back in a fit of rage. The buckle end of a belt. All because I didn't say or do something right, or had disrespected him, or had talked back, or whatever he thought it had to be to give him the permission to do what he so often did to me.

Alcohol on his breath and the smell of a BBQ he had been to without me became his new cologne. And an occasional new and unrecognizable smell sometimes accompanied him home, and yet, when I asked what it was, he never really knew.

Making love in any consensual sense was long gone; I guess it was never quite really there. Kissing was a thing of the past, too, unless he was drunk and really wanted "it." "It," again, consisted of about five minutes or less, with nothing ever pleasurable or satisfying to me.

Maybe the most hurtful thing he ever did to me was when he ordered my cat, Whiskers, to be put down. He was a beautiful Persian cat with long whiskers and huge blue eyes. I adored him. He was my confidant, my consolation. And X loved him too.

Sadly, one day Whiskers developed a common bladder complaint that could have been treated, as the vet explained, with a modified diet, medication and time. But X wasn't listening to the vet or to me, and just ordered that Whiskers be put out of his misery, thereby driving a hole into my heart that took me forever to recover from. X's behavior was all the harder for me to understand because he had been so distressed about Whiskers' illness. Getting the matter over and done with quickly and decisively, rather than helping Whiskers fight his way back to health, must have been his way of dealing with the sorrow he felt – that it was better for Whiskers to die peacefully immediately than for him to suffer any longer, even if it would mean that his life might be saved – but he certainly wasn't taking into account the torture he would be putting me through for the foreseeable future.

Then, one day, I almost got away for good!

Almost …

X had invited some people he knew, strangers to me, to our house for a BBQ. Two men and a woman I had never seen before were in our backyard drinking beer and smoking while they cooked steaks on our grill. I looked out and saw X smoking.

'What in the hell?' I thought to myself. "He doesn't smoke!"

I went outside and asked him what he was doing and he just laughed at me.

He must have told me to go back inside because the next thing I remember was him coming in the house in a rage with a metal rod in his hands, demanding to know why I had humiliated him like that in front of his friends.

"Who the hell do you think you are coming out there and asking me questions?"

He began to chase me around the house, swinging the rod as if to hit me with it. I was terrified.

Even his brother, who lived with us, came out of his room and asked him to stop, but was quickly told where he could go.

X hit the wall and the ceiling, leaving gouges in them. He smacked the potted plants I had in our living room and made a huge mess. It was as if some force had taken over him.

The rest is a blur, but I remember him going back outside, and as I looked out the window again to see where he was, he was laughing with that woman and talking to the guys.

I immediately had the thought to get out, to take my purse and the clothes on my back, and go. I would leave, go into hiding, and call my parents to tell them everything. This was it! If I didn't, I knew it would just be a matter of time before he would kill me. After what I had just seen and been through, I just had to get out.

So I made one last check through the window to see if he was still talking, and he was. Then I went to the phone – there were no cell phones in those days – and called for a taxi to come get me.

I was so nervous and frightened, feeling sick to my stomach at the thought of escape, an escape to final freedom.

It seemed like f o r e v e r before that cab showed up, but it finally did. I was watching for it at the front door and began to walk outside when X came into the house. He saw the cab and put two and two together.

"Where the %#@ do you think you're going?" he demanded.

He made me tell the cab to cancel the pickup and leave. I can't remember what happened next.

Please draw strength from my experiences and know there is hope. Even if you have already left your abusive situation, let my story be a familiar place you can come to, knowing that I share your pain and heartache, your sorrow and despair.

I'm not saying it will heal you or that this is a miracle cure. No. Just that I understand.

What I am saying is that you are not alone and this was never your fault. Nor was it mine. He took an innocent, young and naïve girl, and made her his pawn. He was a true scam artist whom I now believe had an agenda the whole time.

As I near the end of my story, I have just a few more experiences I would like to share because they include amazing examples of divine intervention in among the horror and violence that would ensue. I hope you draw strength from them as well as from what I have already shared with you.

As I said before, and I will repeat once again, there were many, many physical, emotional and verbal encounters between us. Many stories have been left out but those written have been written to the best of my memory. I have written them from the bottom of my heart with rawness and honesty so you can relate to them but also so that you are motivated by them to find hope.

Chapter 19

Date night

We had stopped going out years before, except on our anniversary and that was usually just dinner. Going out and having fun as a couple never happened anymore.

We had tried for almost two years to have children, even getting an infertility expert involved, but never were able to conceive a child.

At some point in our marriage, X began to help set up musical bands and their equipment when they came to town. On one occasion he told me that a band we both really enjoyed was coming. It was still a few weeks away and I was so excited. I really was looking forward to going and seeing them in person. I hoped we would also dance. This was going to be a great date night for us.

X's brother was still living with us at this time and would also help him set up for them to play.

Well, the weekend was here and the band was still on schedule. The evening of the dance came and I began to get ready. My brother-in-law got picked up early by some friends who were also going there to help and then to the dance.

How exciting this was going to be!

I couldn't contain myself any longer. I went and finished getting all dolled up, and thought I looked really pretty. I had a nice outfit, great hair and makeup.

Still in my early twenties, I had the energy and was ready for a long night out of dancing and fun with my husband.

I hadn't noticed what he was doing or what he was wearing because of my excitement, but saw that he was sitting on the couch when I came out all ready to go. I knew he would notice how great I looked and couldn't wait to hear his comments on it.

He looked up and said, "Where the hell do you think you are going?"

I must have misunderstood him, so I asked him, "What?"

And he again said, "Where do you think you are going?"

To which I replied, "Well, to the dance, of course, silly. Let's go!"

"You're not going anywhere," he said, adding, "In fact, *we* are not going."

What?

I was heartbroken and livid all at the same time. I began to cry and told him his brother had just left and was waiting for us, how I had waited, anticipating this evening for so long, and it was finally here. I wanted to go and begged him to take me.

"No," he said again, and my heart sank.

The next thing I recall was us fighting and arguing about it, and me sitting on the couch, crying, and him yelling and pointing his finger at me as he stood above me.

Here, I believe, is another time my mind has blocked most of the events from my memory, but the next thing I do remember was him going into our bedroom and coming back with his semi-automatic handgun in his hand.

He was shaking as he cocked it and put the cold barrel to my forehead.

"Do you want to die, slut?" he screamed along with a torrent of all sorts of other cuss words. "Do you want to die?"

I recall the desperation I felt as I answered his question. "Yes, kill me. I am sick of living this way! Do it and take me out of this misery!"

His hand was still shaking and the barrel was still on my forehead before he retreated.

I have no memory of what happened next or for the rest of the night.

Horrible, isn't it? Yet divine intervention was actually unfolding, without my knowing, before my eyes, an intervention that would not show itself until a few months later.

The next morning, after X left for work, I picked up that rotten gun. 'I'll take that stupid gun of yours and show you what I can do,' I thought to myself.

So I threw it outside in a sand pile we had for some remodeling we were doing around the house, and I made sure to cover it well and kept it there all day. But as evening approached when X would be coming home, I knew I had better get that gun out of the sand pile and back into the drawer.

So I did just that. I cleaned off all the sand and wiped it down and stored it back in the night stand, safely tucked away in the drawer.

He never knew what I had done.

Chapter 20

Monday

Sometime after that, my cousin was up for a visit and the three of them – my cousin, my brother-in-law and X – all worked together during the day.

One particular afternoon, as I was at the mall looking around, X got it into his head to come looking for me. I remember seeing all three of them circling the mall parking lot in his truck, then X got out and walked into the mall.

He started arguing with me and picking a fight, cornering me by a cookie store. He grabbed my arm and was trying to force me outside, trying to get violent with me right there in the mall, when a passerby saw the commotion.

The passerby immediately asked X, "Hey, what do you think you're doing to her?"

To which X replied, "Fuck you, she's my wife. I can do what I want to her. Mind your own business, you son of a bitch!"

I told the nice man that it was OK and that he needed to go, grateful that, even for a brief moment, he had stood up for me, he had had the courage to confront X. I never saw that man again and X let me go.

On his way out, though, X said something like, "This isn't over. I'll see you back home."

That night, when all three of them got home, I was in our bedroom. My cousin and brother-in-law were sitting down watching TV in the living room when X came in and started right back up where he had left off earlier that day.

He was interrogating me, making accusations, and becoming very angry and violent.

He began to toss me around like a rag doll across the bed and against the walls.

At one point he threw me up against the bedroom window, which miraculously did not break.

I was wearing a favorite sleep shirt my mom had given to me years before. It was hot pink with black polka dots, and was very soft after all the years of my washing and wearing it. I loved that t-shirt.

As X continued to throw me around, he attempted to take it off me and it tore. I was so upset! He then grabbed at my underwear, and as he did so, I stopped and turned away from him.

Well, he didn't let go as I kept fighting to get away from him. He was trying to force me into having sex with him.

As I kept trying to get away, screaming at him, my underwear also tore, causing a severe burn mark that wrapped around my hip bone ten inches long.

I was hoping that my screaming would prompt the other two men in the house to come to my rescue, but they never did.

There I stood, humiliated, naked, battered and burned.

He must have stopped at that point because that's as far as my memory goes about this night. I only recall how much pain and exhaustion my body felt as I laid down and cried myself to sleep.

Once again I found myself begging God to let me die, to somehow get me out of this situation, even through death.

Once again, I held my breath for long periods of time, praying I would pass out and not wake up.

Chapter 21

Tuesday

The very next day after this violent encounter, I asked X's permission to go back to the mall and window shop, which he said I could do. I told him I would be done around 7:00 or 7:30 in the evening.

As I was getting ready to leave the mall, it had become dark outside. I reached for my purse to grab my keys before exiting the mall, and as I began to walk outside, someone came up right next to me.

It was X.

He grabbed my arm forcefully and said, "Let's go. You are coming with me."

I didn't understand. What was happening now?

I told him, "You are hurting my arm. What are you doing? What is going on?"

I was ready to go home within the timeframe I had been permitted, so I didn't understand.

He proceeded to show me his truck, parked diagonally in a space close to my car, and demanded I get in.

"But I have my car right over there," I told him.

He didn't care. He forced me into the truck, squeezing and twisting my arm until I got in, jumping right in behind me and starting to drive away from town.

'Where is he going?' I thought as fear and anxiety began to take over my mind.

But visibly I stayed strong. I was not about to demonstrate any weakness or fear that he could detect.

I asked again, "Where are we going?"

He did not reply.

As we began to leave the city limits, I happened to glance at a sign on the side of the road describing two neighboring towns and their distances from our own. My eye caught the one that said thirty-six miles. The direction he was driving in was heading toward an Indian reservation.

I had only been this way once before with X, on a business trip quite a while before, so the road and terrain were not familiar to me at all, especially at night, and it was now about 8:00 pm.

X loved to watch the hit TV show 'Unsolved Mysteries.' I also enjoyed watching the show at that time. All I could think of at that moment were two things: *Stay calm and show no fear to him,* and *Please do not let him drive off this main highway into a side street.* I did not want to end up like the cases I had seen on that show.

As I was thinking these things, I said to X, "Listen, we have been having problems for a few years. Let's get a lawyer and end this marriage amicably and without incident."

At that moment, he pulled out the gun and a paper bag from under the seat, and rolled down his window.

"I have my lawyer right here with me," he declared as he peeled back the paper bag, exposing a bottle of liquor from which he took a swig.

He then proceeded to shoot the gun right out his window into oncoming traffic.

We were on a two-lane highway and I could not believe what I was witnessing. I was terrified.

"What are you doing?" I screamed. "Stop it!"

He continued driving and I tried to stop him by pulling on his arm. Of course he pulled away and told me to shut up and mind my own business.

I started to pray that he would calm down and not turn into any of the side streets, but suddenly he turned off.

'Don't show fear,' I thought. 'Even if I am to die, I will not die showing fear!'

He drove onto a primitive dirt road for about a mile, leading into a thick forest. I had no idea where he was heading. I had never been out there before.

He continued to drive and any dialog by this point is a blur to me. I just remember how I felt.

He finally came to a spot at the base of a mountain, turned the truck around, and stopped. His window was still rolled down, and he still was in possession of his gun. It was cold and very dark outside. It was the end of October.

Suddenly he pointed the gun at me and said, "Get out!"

"What? There could be mountain lions or bears or who knows what else could be out there. Are you crazy?"

"I don't care," he said. "Get out!"

He cocked the pistol and I clearly remember hearing a click. It got stuck! I know it got stuck because he started hitting the thing against the palm of his hand while still pointing it at me.

At that moment I pushed his arms away so his hand was out of his window. As he kept trying to unjam the gun, I opened the passenger door and started to run down the dirt road as fast as I could.

Scared, terrified, and unsure of where I was going, I ran.

The October sky was dark and haunting, the air was crisp, and all I could hear was the sound of random traffic in the distance and my rapid breathing.

When I looked toward the highway, I could see the lights of what appeared to be toy cars buzzing up and down the road.

I had to actually look away from the road I was on in order to see it because of the darkness. I could barely make out the edges of the road by doing so, but I kept running.

Terrified for my life, confused, and with no idea of where I was or where to go, I began running back to the main road.

All of a sudden, I saw the headlights of X's truck start moving in my direction.

"OMG," I thought, "he is going to run me over!"

I immediately turned off the dirt road and into the bushes, running through the rough terrain, hiding and ducking every time his truck got close.

This went on for a very, very long time. I did not have a watch, so I don't know how much time had actually passed. It was cold and dark. I was wearing a thin denim jacket, jean shorts, and flat ankle boots. I was running, surviving on pure adrenaline. My heart was beating out of my chest.

The next thing I knew, I was approaching the frontage road to the highway and was getting close to freedom, I thought, as I had a plan to hitchhike if need be.

As I kept needing to duck and protect myself now from the lights of oncoming traffic so X couldn't find me, I noticed his truck driving up and down the frontage road. He had gone down the road a-ways, then turned around and driven up again, looking for me no doubt.

I ran back into the bushes, praying he had not seen me.

Immediately, I had a very distinct impression enter my mind to start running back into the field and toward the next city, not back to my town. I remembered that milepost sign, the one my peripheral vision had caught as X drove out of the city limits.

'Thirty-six miles away,' I thought. 'I can make that.'

Hiding and ducking in the bushes every time a vehicle drove by, I set out for the next city.

Chapter 22

Codependency

At some point, I looked back in the general direction of where all this began and noticed X's headlights pointing directly onto the base of the mountain, but they appeared to not be moving anymore.

'What is going on now?' I wondered. 'Did he get out of his truck and is he looking for me on foot?'

Fear amplified in me even more intensely now as I kept running.

Looking down at the ground and not really being able to see my footing, I was grateful that, up to this point, somehow I hadn't fallen or tripped or gotten caught on anything.

As I kept moving farther and farther from that mountain, I could still make out the truck's headlights, still not moving.

Suddenly, an intense panic consumed my thoughts. 'OMG, what if he shot himself? NO! Please, no! He has to be OK! He just has to be OK! Please, God, please, God, no! Please don't let him have shot himself!'

A different fear engulfed me at this very moment. Here I was, literally running for my life. Broken, beaten, and terrified, I now feared for his life, his well-being. All of a sudden, consumed with emotion, I could only pray that he was OK.

As I kept going, something in me knew I couldn't turn back. A silent, yet divine, compass within me kept pointing me to keep moving and neither quit nor turn back.

Sound familiar? Why, you may ask, would I care for his well-being at this point? Others might wish he had shot himself and given me a ticket to freedom, but it doesn't work that way in these situations. You see, it doesn't matter what he has done, how he has done it, how many times he did it. We become dependent on them one hundred per cent because our own identities and our own sense of self-worth have become suppressed from our consciousness. Instead, their lifestyle has become our lifestyle, our survival, our identity.

Notice I did not say, however, that these things are gone from us. No, they are still very much within us as these are gifts from God that will never leave us. They get buried, deep down where we no longer feel them, no longer rely on them because we have been programmed by circumstance, by this abuse, to believe they no longer exist. But we are wrong. They still do exist. I promise you they do.

They are the fuel you will need to jet yourself out of this abusive situation once and for all when that time comes.

When that second of opportunity comes your way, and in most cases all you may get is a second, run! Run with your God-given instincts, and know you have it in you because you must survive because you are worth it!

Chapter 23

Light

As I kept running, hiding and ducking, the truck's headlights becoming dimmer in the distance, shock became my new source for fuel.

I was numb. I had been going and going for what seemed like an eternity now. Running parallel to that distant highway, it had become my only source for direction, my only hope.

Then I saw a tiny light in the distance with some sort of a bluish hue to it, as a beacon in the night. Once again, I was inspired to go to this light. It lay between the highway and the base of the mountain, but now quite a ways away.

Distinctly I heard a voice tell me to continue to this light until I could find it, and that is what I did. What could it be?

As a lighthouse welcomes a lost ship at sea back to its safe harbor, I, too, was guided to my safe port. As I approached this light, I started to make out a little house with a fenced yard. Could it be?

I ran faster as my heart began to feel hope again, and as I got closer and closer, yes! It was someone's home. Humble in means, it shone like a bright ray of hope in the middle of this lonely, chilly night.

I got up to the gate, and several dogs started barking incessantly, growling at me, as they should, to protect their home.

I still remember thinking at that very moment, 'After all I have just been through, what is a dog bite at this point?' and I went in.

Most of the events that followed are a blur again, but I do recall the front porch light being on and the front door opening. I don't remember what was said, but I remember a tall, older man wearing a worn cowboy hat standing in the doorway and inviting me in. I say "inviting" because, although I don't remember what he said at that moment, my next memory takes me to a leather recliner where he had me sit while he brought me a glass of water.

A few moments later, a nice, dark-skinned, petite lady walked into the room saying she was his wife. Her name was M. She was a sweet Native American lady.

The conversation must have been me describing my terror as I recall him saying they did not have a phone. He chuckled and said they could drive me up to the next stop, but it would be a few minutes because they had had a long day at work and had just had a few drinks to unwind not all that long ago.

I didn't care. I was so grateful to be in a safe environment with good people. It was warm and inviting.

I do recall asking the time and it was about 10:30 pm. My terror had lasted about three hours but it was still not over. I mentioned to the man that I saw the headlights and what my fears were, and I distinctly remember his comment.

"Well, we can drive by on our way out and see. Maybe the son-of-a-bitch blew his brains out and he's slowly dying. Nothing short of what he deserves."

"No," I pleaded with him, "please just take me to the nearest phone so I can call 911."

I don't know how much time passed or how long I stayed in that nice couple's home, but the time came and we had to go.

We piled into a small Chevy Luv pickup. I think it was white or tan in color, and had a tiny back seat where I sat. I recall it vividly because the man lit a cigarette and I felt I couldn't breathe. It was so cold outside by now that the windows were left up as we drove away, and at this point I didn't even care about breathing some second-hand smoke. I just wanted to go.

As we pulled out of their driveway, I could still see the headlights of X's truck in the distance.

We drove on a dirt road for what seemed like forever and finally reached the highway. As we turned left to head south back to my town, I felt some relief and yet fear still racked my body.

I didn't know if X was dead or alive. What was to happen now? Would he find me and finish me off? I had no idea what lay ahead for me but I was safe for now.

We drove about fifteen miles and reached a gas station on the outskirts of town. Originally they planned on taking me only a few miles away from their home to a nearby store, but the store was closed and no longer had a pay phone outside.

The man pulled into the gas station parking lot. I don't know what was said, but I know I must have expressed extreme gratitude for all they had done for me.

They waited for me as I got out of the truck and wearily walked my exhausted body to the pay phone located next to the station.

Chapter 24

911

As I dialed 911, the operator came on. I don't recall what my plea was to her when she answered, but I am sure I described the horror I had just been through.

I remember her asking me if my name was "----." She asked me again, and I said, "Yes."

She asked me to hang on and not to hang up.

Looking back on that moment, it's kind of surreal to think that I called in, frantic and scared, and she put me on hold for just a few seconds, which at that moment seemed like forever.

She immediately came back on and said, "I'm sorry I had to do that, but we were just about to send out Search and Rescue for you. Are you OK? What is your location? I'm sending out an officer and I'll stay on the line with you until he arrives."

I desperately asked her how she knew to ask my name. "Why was Search and Rescue called?" I asked of her.

You won't believe the next words that came out of her mouth.

"A man, your husband, I assume, called in that he was just trying to scare you but then couldn't find you."

"What?" I screamed. "He is the reason I was out there! *He* took me out there!"

She said he had mentioned that we had had a fight or an argument and he was just trying to scare me.

"Well, it worked!" I told her.

She asked me to stay on the phone just a little longer as the officer pulled into the parking lot. When the couple who rescued me, my gracious heroes of that night, saw him, they drove away.

As the officer got out of his car and walked toward me, the dispatch operator asked me if I wanted to have contact with X. A county sheriff apparently had made contact and located him, still out in the woods, and was escorting him back to town.

"No, absolutely not!" I replied, terrified. "I am scared of him."

As we were getting ready to hang up, the other officer drove by us with X driving his own truck. I can't remember if he was in front of or behind the officer, I just remember the feeling of fear and wanting to hide as they drove by.

The officer who arrived to assist me, seeing me visibly shaken, frightened, and utterly exhausted, held me in his arms and escorted me to his patrol car, where he asked me some questions. He told me they would be putting me up in a hotel for the night under a victim witness program. This is a service offered to victims of domestic violence that can provide several services, such as temporary residence, clothing, and food.

He was such a kind and gentle man, and I can only pray that somehow he knows that I will forever be grateful to him for the care and compassion he showed me that night.

Thank you so much, officer!

When I began my journey of writing this book, I contacted our local police department to see if they still had any record of that night and maybe a record of his name. The dispatcher could not find anything and feared that, as time passed and computer systems had been upgraded to new ones, they had simply deleted all old records and files.

Then, one day recently, he happened to turn up as a customer where I was working and we reconnected. That moment was so emotional and amazing for both of us. We each had tears in our eyes. I told him I was writing a book about my experiences and he would get a copy when it was published. Officer WV will definitely get his copy with all my gratitude for how he treated me that night.

Chapter 25

Blur

The rest of that night, and many days that followed, are a big blur in my life. I remember not going home for about two or three weeks. I remember getting five hundred dollars cash at the ATM and living in a different hotel behind a restaurant, far from my house.

Rumor around town was that X was looking for me and was going to shoot me on the spot, and I had no choice but to go to the local gun store and buy myself a gun, a .38 Special revolver that I carried in my purse at all times.

At the time I drove a brightly colored vehicle and asked a family friend, who worked for the Sheriff's Department, if I could hide my truck in their police lot for a few days until this all settled down. He said it would be OK, and the very day that I was going downtown to park it in a designated spot, I passed X on the road. I was so scared I turned the corner and drove as fast as I could. I don't even know where I went. Eventually, though, I got the car parked.

I traveled by taxi if I needed to go anywhere for the whole time I was in hiding. At one point I needed personal items and clothes, and had a lady police officer escort me back to my house to get a few things. She checked the home first and deemed it safe to go in, but told me to be quick. It looked abandoned.

I quickly gathered a few things and she took me back to my hotel. I stayed in the room and only had contact with the elders of my church and my best friend at that time. Nobody else knew where I was, not even my parents. They had no idea what hell I had been living in for the past ten years or where I even was now. I felt bad for them, so bad, but I had to protect them. If he could do this to me, then what was he capable of doing to them?

I ordered my food from the restaurant next door, usually via room service. Sometimes my friend would pick something up and bring it to me and spend time with me. Other than that, I was in hiding pretty much the whole time.

I went to church a couple times in a taxi, always fearing X might show up during sessions and shoot me or hurt me somehow. The elders of the church were on alert and I carried my gun with me at all times.

It was one of these elders in particular who kept me in the loop as to what was going on with X through things X was saying in town and rumors he was spreading. This same elder was threatened over the phone by X, who landed in jail because of it. I was still in hiding when this took place.

While all this was happening, my parents were desperately trying to get a hold of me, now suspecting something very wrong had happened. They felt this way because, when they called our house, X would not talk to them, and of course I was never there. My brother-in-law consistently lied to them, saying X and I were out on a date or at a movie. My parents knew better.

Somehow, through this elder, my parents and I made contact, and they immediately left their home to drive the ten hours to see me.

When my parents made it to town, only then was I safe to go home. I did, but was still very frightened.

I don't know where X was at this time, but he had requested we talk. The next thing I knew, my parents and I agreed to meet with him, but it had to be in a public location. I would not meet under any other circumstance and my parents had to be there.

So we met for breakfast at a local restaurant and sat at a table for four. I don't remember exactly what was said, but I do remember X pleading with me to take him back, saying how sorry he was. He even shed a tear, which my mother was fooled into believing because she then said to me, "Maybe you ought to reconsider and try again. Give him another chance."

I'll admit, for a split second, it all seemed possible, the fantasy that maybe this whole experience might have changed him. Maybe now we could be happy. On the other hand, this was my way out, my way to be free of all the emotional, verbal, and physical abuse I had not only endured but survived for almost ten years.

"Sorry, Mom, but no, I can't," I told her, then turned to him and said the same thing.

He pleaded his case once again and begged me to forgive him and to take him back.

At that moment I felt release. At that moment fear was not in me, and instead I was filled with a sort of power and strength that gave me the courage to say, "No, it's over."

I know that once again God was by my side.

Chapter 26

A new start

After a few weeks, my father had to go back home and tend to his responsibilities. My mother stayed with me until I established an apartment in town, and she even helped me pack and move in. Things were peaceful, even amicable, but a lingering fear and constant caution were always in the back of my mind.

I was on high alert. I never let my guard down.

So many things happened between the time my parents arrived and when I moved out, and also during the six months before our divorce was final. It was a bitter divorce, but not as nasty as some can be. The judge gave me the house with everything in it, and gave X the business and all that pertained to it.

Of course, X did not obey the judge's order and told me that if I wanted the household items I was awarded, then I needed to pay the remaining debt on them.

"No, thanks," I told him. "I'll only take what I need," as I knew X and the judge were really good friends.

So that is what I did. I took a bed, a dresser, two lamps, two nightstands, my fish, my clothes … and my life. I didn't even keep his last name.

Eventually I sold the house and got screwed in the deal, but that's a story in and of itself.

I avoided X and stayed away from him as much as I could. We crossed paths a few times simply because we lived in the same town, and at some point, through the grace of God, I was given the strength to forgive him.

I heard he eventually lost the business, that he had gotten into some shady deals and had moved away. I don't know where he moved. There were always rumors flying and somehow somebody always knew something or someone who knew where X was. I heard his life got worse and some pretty bad things came his way. Karma? Perhaps. Other than that, I do not know where he is or what he is doing to this day.

All in all, I feel that our final encounters were amicable. We were two souls who simply lost their way through horrific circumstances and miraculously survived. I really hope, for his sake, that he learned from his mistakes and was able to better serve himself and his fellow man. I feel that if it were not for these trials I had to go through during this time in my life, I would not be the person I am today. I have learned a lot, I have grown a lot, and I have been through a hell of a lot.

I am a survivor!

I trust I have brought honor and hope to all you who have had a similar situation in your lives. I offer my sincerest gratitude and love that you have read about my experiences. May God protect you, bless you, and give you the strength and courage you need, as He so graciously gave to me when I didn't even know He was there.

Epilog

About a year after my kidnapping experience, I drove by myself to the spot where I had started running. It is known locally as a sacred place. (There are no coincidences.)

I also drove to M's house to see where all this had happened and to discover just how far it actually was. I had run quite a distance, and I noticed that, had I turned south that fateful night and run back toward town, I probably would not be alive today. There are a couple of cliffs in the landscape as you head through the forest back toward town. In the dark, I could have easily fallen down these, breaking a leg or even worse, and possibly not been found for days.

I learned that M had worked at the local grocery store at which I had been shopping for years, but I hadn't known her. I eventually reconnected with her at the grocery store and we embraced. From then on I called her my guardian angel. She invited me to her home, and I took my mom to meet her and her husband.

After that meeting, on the way back to my apartment, my mom told me something incredible M had shared with her. M had said that, on the very day I knocked on their door, they had just installed the generator that powered the light I had seen that night, that beautiful little blue light.

Remember the gun getting jammed that night in the truck? Do you also remember that I had put the gun in a sand pile in our backyard? I truly believe with all my heart that, if it hadn't been for that sand, the gun would have fired.

Someone, I don't recall who (although it may have the 911 operator), told me that X had fired all the rounds, hoping I would hear them and run back to the truck.

I never heard those shots.

Although he didn't want to, X and I had agreed to take that six-month class before we could marry in the church. As we were attending these classes, one of the first things required of us was to go to confession. As we met the priest at the church one evening, I was chosen to go first. Something inside me told me not to, but to let X go first instead. As he and the priest entered the confessional and the light switched over to red, that same voice told me to kneel at the last pew and to begin praying.

I had no hesitation as I knew my heart was very heavy with much to confess. How could I face this priest and tell him the horrible things I had been through in the past few months, and worst of all, how could I confess to him that horrible tragic day in that big city? I wouldn't.

I was told again to pray, and pray I did. I don't know how long I knelt there, or how long X was in the booth. All I know is that I took that inspiration and opportunity to pour my heart out to God. All of it. I prayed and cried, and prayed and sobbed, and continued to pray, begging, supplicating His forgiveness, praying to be cleansed of my horrible sin and to be given another chance.

All of a sudden I felt a profound shift in my feelings, in my emotions, and in my mind. I was forgiven. He, Almighty God, had somehow forgiven me all my sins.

My body and my spirit were overcome with a warm feeling of calm, a feeling of acceptance, a feeling of peace. I was amazed and I accepted it.

Sometime later X came out and the priest signaled me over. At that moment I felt that I no longer needed to confess to this man. I had confessed directly to God. I think I waived at him and nodded so as to say, "Not today," and we left.

God was there with me all the way. All of it. Through every experience from the very start.

I often asked myself later, when times got really tough, 'Why? Why did I survive, and why did I survive especially that cold night in October?'

I believe that, years later, the answer was given to me very clearly by the Almighty.

I had a new marriage, a new beginning, and, later on, a beautiful child. I had a new hope and restored relationship between myself and my God, and an opportunity waiting, locked away tightly in the recesses of my heart for over twenty-five years, to share my life story with you through this book, to bring honor and glory to our Father in Heaven, and to help you recognize His spirit that is in you, and in all of us, and draw strength and courage through that spirit that you can do anything.

My final return was to the house that X and I had bought, where we had spent the last part of our lives together, where so much abuse and violence had occurred.

My husband and I knocked on the door and the new owner appeared. We explained the situation and she kindly let us in and gave us a tour while I explained something of what had happened there and how I was seeking closure.

I did get closure, but I also got flashbacks. I saw the ketchup on the walls, the potted plants smashed on the floor mixed in with the carton of eggs he also smashed – all for me to clean up.

Then I remembered even darker stuff. How I would try to avoid his aggression by escaping to the bathroom to pee, and he would refuse to let me close the door and just watch me while I went about my business with either a sullen or a menacing look etched across his face. How, one time, he smashed my head against the basin as I was washing away my tears once again from another argument, another act of violence. How he would try to force himself on me while I was in the shower, pretending he wanted to kiss me or to seduce me in the most intrusive of ways, but really reveling in his strength while I was at my most naked and vulnerable, humiliating me, intimidating me, and abusing me.

I didn't tell this nice woman all that I was reliving, but the wounds came back, raw and livid – and then they healed.

And then I healed.

Thank you for listening to me.